Advance Praise

The freedom to just BE! I feel a huge sense of relief from this reminder that I don't have to go out there and conquer the world to feel worthy. I am enough just as I am, and so are you. If you are ready to stop getting burned out from pushing too hard in your life, *Open Your Heart* will help you create a new lifestyle where you lead your life with grace and ease.

~ Natalie Ledwell, Best Selling Author of Never in Your Wildest Dreams
MindMovies.com

If you are a woman who's DONE waiting for permission to live a life on fire + on purpose, this book is a must read. Tanya is the real deal, a feminine leader who walks her talk and speaks her truth with unwavering candor and vulnerability.

~ Lisa Steadman, Author of It's A Breakup, Not A Breakdown
LisaSteadman.com

A New Generation Feminine Leader takes a stand for her freedom by no longer suffering in silence. A woman's voice is one of her greatest assets. This book will empower you to find yours ... and use it.

~ Christina Dunbar, ArtistPreneur, Writer, Performer
ChristinaDunbar.com

Tanya faces love like a blazing dragon and shows us how we can do it too. Opening our hearts is the great call of our time in history. This book unravels the art of expressing love as our profound purpose in life.

~ Laura Hollick, Soul Art Shaman
SoulArtStudio.com

Open Your Heart will heal so many women globally who have given away their power, been hurt in the past or feel ashamed of their mistakes. The wisdom in this book empowers the modern women to shift from being the victim or a martyr and step confidently into leading her life in her truth.

~ Hillary Rubin, Spiritual Life + Business Coach,
Creator of The Art of Becoming A Coach Training Program
HillaryRubin.com

Imagine if every woman accepted herself ... then every child would watch their mother and learn how to be at peace with themselves. The world would be filled with children who feel empowered to be themselves. *Open Your Heart* will create a new world of people who follow their hearts' desires.

~ Laura Plumb, Ayurvedic Consultant and Health Writer
Food-ALoveStory.com

Open Your Heart is a must read for all women. It is a rallying cry for the feminine. It will inspire you, make you cry and give you a hope for the next generation. If you are looking for an empowering book to be the woman you've always wanted to be, this is it!

~ Megan Kennedy, Human Resources

Awake since 4 am ... this is exactly what I need to hear today. Bowing down to the channel that is you and the divine coming through ... I am listening.

~ Paula Argentieri James, UC Berkeley Professor

Tanya Lynn is the real deal. She writes like she talks ... eloquent, poetic, inspiring and raw. If you are looking for a role model who embodies the teachings and demonstrates leadership, look no further than this woman. *Open Your Heart* is a vulnerable and authentic journey of a woman who has truly integrated her feminine and masculine qualities to be a new generation feminine leader.

~ Rose McPherren, Body Psychologist

Finally a feminist book that focuses on women stepping into their feminine to inspire and empower men and children as well as themselves. This book gives a holistic model to change the world. A true winner!

~ Lucia Evans, Coach

I devoured *Open Your Heart*. . . The concepts and exercises were so right on for me! The invitation to dance and express my joyful freedom is brilliant. I will never look at my life the same way again. I highly recommend this book.

~ Chandra McAtee, HHP Educations Specialist

Open Your Heart will do exactly that: help you fall in love with yourself, your sisters and the world.

~ Sonia Reece, Vibrant Soul Therapy

Tanya Lynn is a change agent. She is willing to walk into the fire and bare her own heart and soul before she ever asks anyone else to. She is a truth teller and a courageous warrior slaying through the defenses that keep us small and in fear.

~ Suzanne Hanna, Founder of The Wilderness Walk

Beautiful. Extraordinary work. *Open Your Heart* will inspire many women to move through hurt, shame and the places where they don't feel safe to share their full selves. And from this place, they may shine as the true leaders they are meant to be.

~ Sharla Jacobs, Co-Founder of Thrive Academy
Thrive-Academy.com

One of the most difficult things is being vulnerable and sharing your heart in fear of getting hurt. Tanya brilliantly makes it look easy and inspires women to open their hearts and tell the truth. This is how we will change the world.

~ Brigit Esselmont, Tarotpreneur & Intuitive Reader
BiddyTarot.com

Open Your Heart

How to be a New Generation
Feminine Leader

TANYA LYNN

New Fem Publishing

email: admin@sistershipcircle.com

www.Sistershipcircle.com

Cover Design: Lucinda Kinch

Ordering Information:
Quantity sales. Special discounts are available on quantity purchases by corporations, associations, and others. For details, contact the publisher at the address above.

Dedication

To all my tribe sisters who believe in the power of sisterhood:
You sit in circle and allow yourself to be seen, fully, all parts.
You are not afraid to get messy, raw and vulnerable.
You know you are safe because your sisters have your back.
Never stop telling your truth.

Second Edition Note

Six weeks before Open Your Heart's book launch in 2014, I took 12 women through a beta 6-week journey using the PlayBook. The women loved it so much that they wanted to continue, and together we co-created the second half of what is now known as Sistership Circle's 12-Week Circle Experience.

It changed everything.

I met my now-husband a couple weeks before the book launch and he helped me build out the vision. We renamed the organization from Tribal Truth to Sistership Circle and expanded it globally over the next 3 years.

I knew I needed to come out with the book's second edition since Tribal Truth no longer existed, but I struggled to make it a priority while running the company with a toddler in tow and pregnant with my second.

Finally, during the 40th week of my second pregnancy, while I had nothing else to do but wait for the birth, I pulled it all together. I decided to keep the book in its original content as much as possible except for a few changes:

All references of Tribal Truth have been changed to Sistership Circle where appropriate. The values and essence of the organization is the same even though we now focus on training women to facilitate women's circles.

I edited the second section of the book to reflect my current view on building tribe based on my experience over the past 3 years since writing the original edition.

You'll also notice at the end of each chapter is a Sister Spotlight Story. I invited women who had completed The 12-Week Circle Experience to contribute their stories so that the book reflects not only my voice, but that of the collective sisterhood.

In sistership,
Tanya Lynn

July 24, 2017
Carlsbad, CA

Table of Contents

Introduction

"Upon suffering beyond suffering; the Red Nation shall rise again and it shall be a blessing for a sick world. A world filled with broken promises, selfishness and separations. A world longing for light again. I see a time of seven generations when all the colors of mankind will gather under the sacred Tree of Life and the whole Earth will become one circle again. In that day there will be those among the Lakota who will carry knowledge and understanding of unity among all living things, and the young white ones will come to those of my people and ask for this wisdom. I salute the light within your eyes where the whole universe dwells. For when you are at that center within you and I am that place within me, we shall be as one."

~ Chief Crazy Horse, Sept 1, 1877

We are close to being seven generations – 140 years – after Crazy Horse spoke this prophesy at Paha Sapa with Sitting Bull, four days before he was assassinated.

Seven generations.

Oren Lyons, Chief of the Onondaga Nation, writes: "We are looking ahead, as is one of the first mandates given us as chiefs, to make sure and to make every decision that we make relate to the welfare and well-being of the seventh generation to come … What about the seventh generation? Where are you taking them? What will they have?" [1]

We are in a time right now where we can change the trajectory of humanity. We are on the brink of disaster where we may go extinct before the seventh generation to come. This is a time for our "tribe" to come together as one, to face the truth and ask ourselves:

How will we sustain this planet for our children?

Women, it is up to us. The divine feminine is rising and calling our names. It is our time to take care of the great mother, our earth. To respect, honor, and nurture Her. And the best way to do that is to take care of ourselves. This is an inside job. Coming home to ourselves, the feminine. Respecting, honoring and nurturing ourselves.

This is the new generation feminine leader.

She trusts despite being burned, hurt and shamed.

She takes a stand for her freedom by no longer suffering in silence.

She receives graciously and allows the process to unfold.

She understands the power of being present in the moment, listening to her internal guidance.

She knows that her beauty and strength lies in her vulnerability, asking for help and accepting contribution from others.

A new generation feminine leader has no apologies for displaying her raw emotions, no fear of being seen, and no shame in expressing her voice.

I am a new generation feminine leader.

I draw my line in the sand and declare that *the ancestral feminine wounding stops with me.*

No more "Be like a boy."
No more "Don't be sexual."
No more "Your opinion doesn't count."
No more "Stay silent."
No more "Work hard like a man."
No more "Be a good girl."
No more "Your parents know what's best for you."
No more "Please others."
No more "Be ashamed of yourself."

Stop rubbing stones on her emerging breasts to keep them flat. Stop the genital mutilation. Stop the rape. Stop pouring acid on her face. Stop suppressing, violating and abusing the feminine. The madness stops with me.

The women in the next generation will no longer have this pain and suffering that I have carried from my mother, who carried it from her mother, who carried it from her mother, seven generations deep. For when I am empowered in my voice, in my skin, and in my purpose, I empower other women to speak up, feel unconditionally and dream big. For when I give myself permission to be myself, I give permission to other women to express their truth.

I am part of a new generation. I make my own choices. I lead my own life in truth. And so do you. Can you feel it? Will you own it?

You are a new generation feminine leader. And I'm about to show you how to personify, express and engage as a new generation feminine leader through core principles surrounding *tribe*, as well as embodied practices such as inquiry journaling and affirming rituals.

Creating the Container

Imagine you just walked into a Sistership Circle gathering for the first time. You are a little nervous because you've never been to one. Your friend told you to go, and you see her talking to someone on the other side of the room. You don't want to bother her so you go into the kitchen to grab a cup of tea and start talking with the woman who is hosting the gathering. This is her house. You like that this is at a house because it feels intimate and safe. Suddenly, you hear a chime three times. The women begin to go into the living room and sit in a circle. You go up to your friend, give her a big hug and sit down next to her.

As the leader of this gathering, it is my responsibility to set the example, which means I will be vulnerable and show all parts of myself. I will share my story with you. I will not hold back, for you are my sister. And even though we just barely met in the kitchen, we have known each other for many lifetimes. I know you as your essence. And you know me as my soul.

When we open our hearts and speak what's really going on for us, we truly see each other. We connect from our shared experience of the human condition. We can feel the pain from the journey. We can inspire each other with stories of triumph, how we overcame obstacles and kept going forward, one step at a time. We are two souls on the same path. Searching. Seeking.

This conversation is an opportunity. It showed up at the perfect time. There is no coincidence we meet now on this part of your journey. There will never be another meeting like it, and yet there will be many more experiences so similar. When we open our hearts to one another and share, a deep intimacy is created. A door is unlocked. Our lives will never be the same. When we see the mirror in one another, we have a glimpse of our own soul. We have a spark of recognition that we are one and the same. We are connected.

Sit with me. I'll go first so you feel comfortable sharing your deepest secrets, those parts of yourself that you are afraid to share because you may be judged. Let me show you that there is nothing to fear, nothing to be ashamed of.

I will put myself out there so you can feel my heart. I will speak my truth with vulnerability because I know this is the only way for us to stop hiding our essence or pretending we've got everything put together nicely in a little package.

I'm here to open my heart and tell the truth of my experience as a new way of interacting with you, a stranger. We are part of the same family, the same tribe: humanity. We share the same basic need and desire for love. To feel and experience pure love. Unconditional love, acceptance and understanding. I am here to tell you it is possible to change our experience from one of fear to one of love. And this is the way…

Setting the Intention - Calling in the Four Directions

Every tribe has its rituals. If you look at rituals like football tailgating, Sunday brunch and Thanksgiving dinner, you can see a common theme: bonding. Rituals create culture. They create connection. They become sacred.

However, there is something missing in some of the modern day rituals. We are, as a whole, a modern tribe who has lost our connection with the *earth*. We forgot who Mother Earth is for us. We forgot where home is. We forgot how to draw on the medicines of the land and live in harmony with nature.

We are in a unique time right now where we have access to wisdom from ancient cultures and traditions and can integrate them into our modern day experience. It is not too late. We simply need to remember who we ARE. We start this book with a ritual from the Native Americans, "Calling in the Four Directions."

As you read this aloud, find a compass and face each direction with at least one hand up to receive the energy from that direction in the palm of your hand. Soak up the intention from each direction and bring that energy into your body through your hands, which are powerful conduits.

To the NORTH:

To the element of Earth, the time of the New Moon, and the season of Winter, the time of midnight each night … the time when the outer world is the darkest and we must go within to find our own light. Thank you for the wisdom that comes from experiencing the darkness and the blessings that come from touching the center of our own being. We embrace the times of quiet, stillness, and seeming stagnancy in the dead of winter, and trust that the light always returns just like the sun, the moon, and the Springtime. We trust and hold that we are unconditionally supported … even in the darkest of nights. We honor the energy of the STILLNESS and DARKNESS of the NORTH.

We call in INTROSPECTION. When the outer world is dark we go within to call forth our inner light. We open our hearts to the pain and suffering of the world. We honor all parts of ourselves.

To the EAST:

To the land of the rising sun, the element of Air, the time of the crescent moon, the season of Spring, and the dawn of the new day … We are deeply grateful for each new day you give us. Thank you for the warmth of the sun, for the continual ability to rebirth ourselves, and for inspiration and great thoughts that move through us in consistently new and beautiful ways. We trust in the regeneration of life and in the cycle that all life and creativity must endure – of death and rebirth, time and time again. We celebrate today the time of coming back into being, and honor the return of LIFE in its FULLNESS in the EAST.

We call in INSPIRATION from the rising sun. We give our listening generously to others. We are receptive to what the universe offers. We honor a commitment to live life to the fullest.

To the SOUTH:

To the element of Fire and the time of the Full Moon, to the Season of Summer and noontime each day … We are deeply grateful for the strength to take ACTION and EXECUTE our thoughts into fruition. We celebrate this time of intensity and illumination so that we may see what needs to be seen, and do what needs to be done. Let our souls be fueled by the fire of PASSION and DEDICATION to what matters, and help us to take action and fulfill that which our hearts ache for most. We honor the energy of ACTION in the SOUTH.

We call in DETERMINATION. We celebrate this time of intensity and illumination so that we may see what needs to be seen, and do what needs to be done. Let our souls be fueled by the fire of PASSION and DEDICATION to what matters, and help us to take action and fulfill that which our hearts ache for most.

To the WEST:

To the element of Water and the time of the waning crescent moon, to the Season of Autumn, the time of Dusk each day. To the ABILITY to TRUST the flow of our emotions. We are grateful today for times of transition, change, and uncertainty, knowing these times have the power to birth great STRENGTH and COURAGE within. We thank you for the PATIENCE we hold for ourselves and others as we all flow with the ups and downs of life. We know that emotions and experiences will come and go, and we open ourselves to the love, acceptance, and peace that come from this understanding. We honor the energy of CHANGE and FLOW in the WEST.

To the CENTER:

We call in UNITY, ACCEPTANCE and CONNECTION as one tribe. As we all face one another and meet in the center, we build our container for safety.

~ From Tribal Truth's Honoring The Masculine gathering, credit to Laura Swan for compiling

Why You Want Tribe

Everyone wants *tribe*. We want to feel like we belong, like we've found our people. It's a sense of coming home. We want to feel safe, comfortable and secure in who we are, so we gravitate toward people who are like us. They look like us, have the same belief systems, values and upbringing. They think like us and sometimes talk like us.

Two important issues come with tribe:

The first is that because they (tribe) are like us, they mirror all parts of ourselves. This can be so confronting, because we don't want to see the parts we don't like about ourselves. We blame others instead of seeing the reflection. We point the finger and disconnect to avoid facing any pain and discomfort.

The second issue is when we find our tribe, we launch a trajectory towards separatism. First, we claim ownership through identification and label our tribe, distinguishing it from the others. Then we want to make sure we made the right choice and ensure our safety, so we validate. In order to validate our tribe, we compare it to other tribes, and we look for what makes our tribe better. Suddenly, we see the other tribe as a threat, competition, and the enemy.

So why do we want *tribe* again? Because of the fundamental truth that we are all connected. All of us. Everything. And we want to have that feeling of connection, to know that we are not alone, to know that we are part of something greater. It gives us a sense of purpose and meaning, a feeling of fulfillment.

To create connection, we must allow ourselves to be seen – all parts of ourselves. And yet this is so scary, because when we reveal our true essence as opposed to the identity we created for ourselves, we risk judgment. We risk being thrown out. But what I have found is the opposite.

When I've told the truth about my feelings, I've felt more connected.

When I've told the truth about the lies I told in the past, I've been forgiven.

When I've told the truth about my resistance, I've opened up doors for freedom.

When I've told the truth about my fears, I've broken through my glass ceiling.

When I am most vulnerable, I am actually the most safe. When I am most vulnerable, I have come into my power by having the courage and strength to tell the truth. I create safety for myself and, in the process, for others.

And when I am confident to tell the truth – *when it becomes more natural to speak up than be silent, stand up instead of be pushed down, own my power instead of give it away* – I have a new capacity to lead my own life, create my desired lifestyle, live out my purpose and feel fulfilled.

I can *speak boldly* that I have a dream and *stand confidently* that I can make it a reality.

Our deepest desires and dreams inside our hearts are realized when we stop holding back the truth. Speaking the truth is access to living a life filled with freedom, abundance, joy and love. It is also access to living in real tribe.

When we accept and love all parts of ourselves – through truth telling – we can also accept and love all parts of the people around us, including the garbage truck driver, the homeless man and the criminal.

If we want to see peace in the world, we have to stop identifying other people as the enemy and as competition. We have to start seeing ourselves as one united tribe on the planet, beautiful in its diversity, inspiring because of its differences, magnificent in its paradoxes.

There will always be darkness, otherwise there will be no light. There will always be sadness so we can recognize the joy. What we must understand is this ebb and flow of nature; the change of seasons; the shift from day to night. What we must master is *stillness* to be calm in the midst of the storm, *awareness* to remember and shed light on the truth, and *communication* to bring us together as one harmonious community.

We all have a dream, and that dream ultimately comes down to happiness; to do what we love, be around people we love, and be in love with ourselves. The dream fulfillment is living an integrated, whole life, such that your work, your relationships and your spirit are all in alignment.

At Sistership Circle, we aim to create a culture where we stand for one another to have our dreams fulfilled. We are a tribe who cares about the state of the planet and humanity. We see the potential of coming together in collaboration to make the necessary shift where everyone wakes up to their full potential and lives it. We are a tribe who sees it as absolutely critical that we integrate the masculine and feminine.

Celebrating the feminine essence rising–
the intuitive, sensual, receptive, connected flow and power.

Inspiring and empowering the masculine–
the strong and determined protector and provider.

We are a tribe conscious about what we put on and in our bodies. We are a tribe who stands for one another's brilliance, especially in times when we cannot see it for ourselves.

There is power in real community that stands for something. Our purpose is to continue to stand when no one else is standing. To be the rock that humanity needs right now. To embody co-creation and collaboration. To be one. Connected. Whole. Fulfilled.

Sistership Circle is a well for each of us to come to when we are thirsty and fill our cup so that it is overflowing with abundance. We give from this place to the rest of the world.

This truth telling is not an easy path. Being in real community is cutting edge, some say even a little before our time. It brings up old wounds and new pains, and yet the rewards are so great, the healing so powerful and the love so immense. Being in real community, or belonging to tribe, is the opportunity of our lifetime.

Will you open yourself to receive this opportunity?

From Martyr to Leader

I've been the martyr, sacrificing myself in the name of helping others. I've spent my whole life working hard to be a contribution in the world. I've been telling myself that I will be worthy of receiving if I keep giving more and more and more at the expense of my own health and sanity.

It's a lie.

The truth is that there is no changing the world; there is simply being in it and accepting it. Stop the over-doing. Start taking care of yourself. There is a reason they tell you to put the oxygen mask on yourself first before helping the person next to you. If your tank isn't filled, if you aren't taking care of your own wellbeing, if you aren't honoring yourself first and foremost, you are simply repeating the old pattern of "not enough" that has been consuming the planet.

What's consuming our planet is the constant need for bigger and more to compensate for the feeling of internal lack and unworthiness. Bigger cars, bigger homes, bigger Big Macs. More money, more electronics, more Facebook friends.

Rather than bigger and more, how about truth and passion? People are seeking the truth. Why are we here? What's the point of it all?

Is there meaning in what I do? Am I fulfilled? What does my heart desire? More and more people are leaving traditional nine to five jobs and pursuing their passions, taking a leap of faith to use their 401K now instead of waiting until retirement.

They are seeking spiritual practices and self-development courses to increase awareness and find inner peace. Yoga and meditation are now mainstream. The eco-friendly green movement is in full force and people see the benefit of eating vegetarian or even vegan. Celebrities flaunt their Prius cars and green juices. It's cool to belong to a co-op or community garden. More businesses are choosing sustainable, conscious practices as their employees demand it.

It's about time we see our potential as spiritual beings in human bodies. It's about time we claim back our power and start standing up for a harmonious world where we value people, profits and the planet equally.

But are we really waking up? And is it too late? The statistics around the problems we are facing are staggering:

Climate
Carbon dioxide, or CO_2, is released by burning fossil fuels to provide the energy that drives almost every aspect of modern life. It has a long life in the atmosphere, so the build-up of heat-trapping gas is cumulative. Scientists have said that the safe limit of carbon in the atmosphere is somewhere between 250 and 450 parts per million (ppm). Already at 390 ppm, levels are steadily rising. The temperature-regulating mechanisms that have been operating for hundreds of thousands of years have been disrupted.

Species
Five times in the Earth's geological history, mass extinctions occurred. The last known time this happened was when the dinosaurs became extinct 65 million years ago. Now it is happening again, on an even larger scale. As a result of human impacts, the current rate of extinction is 100 to 1,000 times higher than average.

Food

Right now enough food is produced for everyone on Earth to be fed adequately. Yet every night over two billion people go to bed hungry because they cannot afford to buy the food they need.

The major causes of soil degradation include deforestation, over-exploitation for firewood, overgrazing, agricultural activities, and industrialization.

40% of the globe's farmlands are degraded, and 20% are in danger of becoming deserts.

The loss of freshwater reserves and the loss of topsoil have been decreasing worldwide yields for many staple crops.

> *"The nation that destroys its soil, destroys itself."*
> **~ Franklin Delano Roosevelt**

Population

Humans currently number about 7 billion. This number is projected to exceed 9 billion by mid-century. The trajectory of population growth is unsustainable. It took all of human history until 1830 for world population to reach one billion. The second billion was achieved in 100 years, the third billion in 30 years, the fourth billion in 15 years, and the fifth billion in only 12 years.

Pollution

Every day, the U.S. throws "away" 600 million plastic bottles. That's 219 billion bottles thrown "away" in America each year.

Poverty

"Residents of slums, while only 6 percent of the city population of the developed countries, constitute a staggering 78.2 percent of urbanites in the least-developed countries; this equals fully a third of the global population." ~ Mike Davis [2]

Here is another staggering statistic: We are using up five times the resources of the planet. We are on the brink of global catastrophe as has been evident by the long list of natural disasters of 2012 alone:

North American Derecho. North American Drought. African Sahel Regional Drought. Middle East Earthquakes. Asian Earthquakes. Global Flooding. North American Heat Wave. Oklahoma and Washington State wildfires. Colorado Wildfires. Tornados in Poland, Japan, Indonesia, and Turkey. U.S. Tornados. Afghanistan Avalanches. Siachen Glacier Avalanche. Pacific Typhoon Season. Cyclone Nilam. Hurricane Ernesto. Hurricane Isaac. Hurricane Sandy. And the list goes on ...[3]

This so-called "problem" out there in the external world is a **reflection of the internal psyche of humanity**. We so desperately want to belong. To know we are worthy. To feel adequate enough to be loved.

We numb out. We check out. We disconnect. We don't want to feel the anger, grief or shame.

We seek approval. We aim to please. We try so hard to look good and cover up any insecurities or flaws that may cause rejection. We wave our arms frantically to grab someone's attention – anyone's – just to feel love.

Love is a choice. Love is within. Love is a courageous act of letting go of fear, lack and scarcity.

Today I let go of all of it. I have nothing to prove anymore. I don't need to be, look or act a certain way. Quite frankly, I don't have to do anything to fit in.

Today I go internal and feel. *All of it.* And in feeling my emotions I feel the rest of humanity. I cry not just for myself, but for you, too. I cry with compassion for our condition. I cry for our pain. And I cry for the freedom we all seek – freedom from this suffering, freedom from these confines we set for ourselves. I cry with the knowing that this too shall pass because moment by moment, life is changing. I am changing. I cry with relief that I don't have to make a difference to have you see me.

Because when I finally stop and allow myself to be seen – really seen in my vulnerability – I get confirmation from your nod and the look in your eye that yes, I fit in, I belong, and I am just like you: a human BEING. There is nothing to do. Nothing to fix. Nothing to change. Nothing to save. May the martyr rest in peace.

So then, if I am not the martyr nor the victim nor my identity nor my ego, **Who Am I?** Is it at all real? Or is it just a dream?

What is a life worth living?

You want to live this life to the fullest.

You want to live a life of least effort and maximum flow.

You want to know that at the end of the race, you can say that you gave it your all.

You don't regret it, you didn't waste it.

A life worth living is one that is in full alignment with your heart's desires. You are living in alignment with truth, which ultimately comes down to:

- Being a fully embodied grown woman; not a child trapped by the voice of your mother and father echoing in your head, policing your every move.

- Being so in tune with the universe that you can manifest whatever you want whenever you want.

- Being self-responsible and self-reliant such that you think, feel and act for yourself.

- Being a conduit for the divine to work through you, so your work is your dharma.

- Being free to grow, expand, explore and play in this beautiful life.

Ultimately, this comes down to one thing: Being the new generation feminine LEADER; a woman who leads her own life and **allows joy** knowing she is infinitely **abundant.** Not chasing money, because you know that you have everything you need in every given moment. Not pursuing happiness because you allow joy to penetrate your open heart.

As you lead your own life, you naturally share your merits, wisdom and experience with those around you. You impact those around you simply by who you are being. They want what you have. They gravitate toward you.

To be a true leader requires partnership and collaboration from your tribe of women and men, a convergence of sisterhood and brotherhood in an integrated family where we celebrate our differences.

That word leadership may scare you. *Don't let it.* I'm not talking about leadership as a role in society, like the President of the United States of America or the CEO of a Fortune 500 company. Leadership is:

- Leading your own life.

- Gaining the awareness and wisdom to see the perfection in every moment.

- Trusting yourself because you have what you need to fully let go of the pretense and simply be.

- Trusting that others are on their path and by staying on yours, you can inspire.

- Taking ownership, responsibility and integrity to stand in the truth of your own experience and trusting your inner guidance.

- Leading your own life in alignment with the **truth** of your experience.

Here's what I mean by truth. We are all reflections and mirrors and projections. We are all connected. We are all one. Love is all that is real. The opposite of love is fear, which is an illusion. All fear-based thoughts are not real. You have a choice in every moment to choose love and expand or choose fear and contract. Think loving thoughts. Speak loving words. Take loving action. Love thyself. Love others.

Every single person on this planet is here for a purpose: to keep remembering the truth of who you are. Your job is to keep following the flow of your life. To notice the coincidences. To watch for the clues. You have been given unique talents and gifts and have developed skills from your unique path to guide you toward fulfilling your part in the big puzzle called life. To create harmony, just like nature's ecosystem, each person has their own individual work that complements the work of others and contributes to the whole.

You are perfect, whole and complete. There is nothing wrong with you. There is nothing to fix, change, convert or heal. All there is for you to do is *be*. Accept. Allow. Love.

Telling the truth will set you free ...
telling the truth will change the world.

Leadership has gotten a bad rap, yet it is the most important thing on the planet right now. One misconception about leadership is that it requires a lot of work. Another misconception about leadership is that there are only a few who have what it takes to be a leader.

The new model of leadership has nothing to do with titles, careers, politics, accolades, or accomplishments. The new model of leadership is for the everyday woman on her journey. The new model of leadership is for the everyday man on his path. The new model of leadership is based on YOU leading your life with vulnerability, in naked exposure, with nothing to hide.

Are you ready to lead your own life with effortless flow? Are you willing to open your heart and lean in to *collaborate* and *connect* with the people around you in your neighborhood and across the globe?

Imagine a life of play, adventure and exploration. Imagine the places you'd go, the people you'd meet, the relationships you'd form, the experiences you'd have. Relationships are so critical to our lives. We are not in a vacuum.

There is a huge Opportunity for all of us right now:

- To be in alignment.
- To be in complete flow with the universe.
- To co-create and collaborate as our natural expression.
- To be one. Connected. Whole.

When you own your power, take the woman's hand to your left and the man's hand to your right, and then co-create together from a place of strength and abundance, something magical happens. Possibilities are endless. A new culture emerges.

It is our time to come together as a tribe. And yet, we have not been taught by society to work together as one tribe. Our egos keep us separate, alone and in fear. Our lives get busier and busier and we quickly forget about our vision and our inspiration.

These three questions become pivotal points in our exploration:

How do we create community that sticks together through thick and thin?

How do we handle our upsets and frustrations with one another when they come up?

How do we embrace the darkness when all we want is the light?

The answers to our pivotal questions frame a new lifestyle, a new paradigm. You have full permission to screw up, fail, crash and burn. You have full permission to forgive yourself when you do so. And you have full permission to love your sisters and brothers despite their imperfections and mess-ups.

We are a tribe of people developing a culture and a movement through our interactions with one another. Many people don't really get it. We may be a little ahead of our time and it's cutting edge, as I said earlier. And yet day-by-day, person-by-person, the love spreads.

How do we create this new culture? I believe the answer lies in **empowering women, unconditionally loving our children and partnering with our men. When we do these three things we create a feminine container to hold the world that inspires and empowers the divine masculine.**

Empowering Women

Empowering women means encouraging and actually holding space for them, to claim their feminine power back and come to a place of embracing both their feminine and masculine qualities. When women can love and accept all parts of themselves, they find their voice. When they find their voice, they take action and don't tolerate the things in the world that create harm to people and the planet.

If women stood up and took action together:

- Every child would be fed non-GMO, organic fruits and vegetables. [4]

- Every atomic bomb would be dismantled.

- Doctors would focus on preventable medicine to keep people healthy.

- Politicians would sit in circle to collectively create solutions instead of pushing their agendas and declaring war on one another.

- Businesses would equally prioritize people and the planet with their profits.

- Society would actively choose free energy and dismantle the oil industry.

Idealistic? Yes. A long shot? Probably. Possible? Absolutely.

There is one woman who has inspired me to know in my heart what is possible when women stand together: the Nobel Peace Prize winner, Leymah Gbowee, a peace activist in Africa. In her masterpiece, *Mighty Be Our Powers*, she demonstrates the power of sisterhood in coming together to stop the war in Liberia.

Leymah and her sisters marched into the president's meeting and demanded they sign a peace treaty. Her conviction, strength and perseverance made a huge impact. The men listened.

We can still take action from our feminine and embody the warrioress. Being feminine does not mean sitting around. The action is inspired by the feminine essence, the beingness.

When we take action inspired by our feminine, there is an unparalleled strength that has so much intentional power behind it that the world shifts. This is the difference between masculine forcing and feminine power.

Unconditionally Loving Our Children

What I mean by unconditionally loving our children is teaching them that they are enough just as they are, giving them the freedom to *be* themselves, cultivating self-love and self-acceptance. The education system today is a prison system. It creates docile, obedient workers for the system. It stifles creativity and self-expression.

We need to educate children:

- To find their strengths and follow their passions.
- To collaborate in teams and honor one another's differences.
- To express their creativity and do the things that make them happy.
- To give and receive love.
- And most importantly, to learn that there is nothing wrong with them.

Our children don't need drugs and medication to sit at a desk all day and listen to someone lecture. It's okay to run and scream and skip and jump and laugh and dance and sing and paint and write and play.

Partnering with Men

We must not leave half of humanity behind. As women become empowered and enlightened, they no longer see how men fit into their lives in the traditional sense of the definition that men exist to "provide, protect and procreate." Many women have their own financial security and are not rushing to have children. These empowered women are wondering when a man will meet them on this new playing field, and the men are scratching their heads thinking that the old way of providing and protecting no longer stands true for the modern woman. A gap needs to be bridged. We need a new way of communicating and partnering with one another. We cannot exist without one another.

How do we do this? How do we empower women? How do we unconditionally love our children? How do we create partnership with our men?

Introducing an Open-Hearted Model of Leadership

For the past seven years, I have been exploring a model that I call Co-Creative Leadership. It is an integrative model that starts with opening our hearts to love and acceptance, which allows for creativity and self-expression, and channels collective power through collaboration.

Leadership in today's society is based on authority and power over people. Co-Creative Leadership is based on leveraging collective power. Instead of a hierarchical pyramid structure, it focuses on the circle of life, a wheel where each person is a spoke, equally important and equally needed to move the wheel forward.

How does this open-hearted model of leadership work?

- It gives the power back to the people to work in partnership and collaboration from the place of "I am enough" and "there is nothing wrong."

- It balances the masculine and feminine energies in the world by cultivating both in each of us.

- It shines a flashlight to illuminate the darkness in the world instead of turning a blind eye.

- It is the merging of BEING and DOING – focusing equally on the internal and external: self-reflection and taking action.

We are all leaders. Leaders of our own lives. Leaders in our families. Leaders in our communities. Leaders in the world. Every one of us has the ability to lead.

Imagine if we all took personal responsibility and accountability in our lives, no longer playing the blame and shame game. That's Co-Creative Leadership – open-hearted and pure of spirit.

Look at leadership as an experience, a process where we open our hearts and tell the truth.

Look at Leadership as a Dance

Dancing may seem scary because you think: "I don't know how to dance" or "dancing is hard." Dance, to me, is the expression of the soul. I had wanted to take up dance for a while but felt so much resistance to it. I had memories of quitting ballet at five years old and not being as good as my friends in high school. I didn't feel graceful or sexy. I remember learning salsa in South America and feeling awkward, clumsy and stocky next to the slender teacher. My legs look too short and my torso not thin enough. *Not enough.*

I had this desire to start dancing and I didn't know how to get started because I didn't want to take lessons and pay for them. So I started going to Ecstatic Dance. What I love about Ecstatic Dance is the free flow, dance by yourself or with a partner in silence, wear a blindfold if you want, do-your-thing-and-go-crazy mentality of the event. No one judges you. No one gives two hoots what you look like.

When I first attended, I felt awkward. My movement felt stiff. I held back my expression because I felt self-conscious. I didn't know a lot of people. Some people were slithering on the floor while others were moving in sync back to back with a partner.

As months passed, I started to learn people's names. I learned Contact Improv, where you move in sync with someone else skin to skin. I learned how to move at my own rhythm and not care what anyone thought of me. My body felt fluid. My head no longer stiffly sat on my shoulders, but instead would move with the music. I felt happy. I felt alive. *My heart was open.*

I didn't go to dance with a man or in a group. I went to dance by myself; every once in a while I would come into contact with another person and we would dance together, then move away.

Dance became an expression of my emotions. It allowed me to access my self-expression in a fun and playful way. The link between Co-Creative Leadership and dance is remarkable.

Rules of the Dance:

- One person leads, the other follows; it can switch at any time, as long as it is communicated.
- Both people follow their intuition and feel the other person until they get into sync with one another.
- The less thinking, the more feeling, the more fluidity and flow in the dance.
- There are steps involved, but the beauty comes from the graceful way the partners move with one another when they are in magnetic attraction.
- Both are equally responsible for knowing the steps, trusting and leaning in.
- The dance does not work unless both partners are committed and fully present.
- The dance starts with YOU.

In dance, you allow spirit to move through and guide you. For most people who do Ecstatic Dance, it is a spiritual practice of divine flow. It is an embodied experience of Spirit.

Dance is a co-creation with the divine and then a co-creation with a partner, which is exactly what Co-Creative Leadership embodies.

Before we delve deeper into tribe in the coming chapters, I invite you to dance. (There is always movement at the beginning of the gathering.) Drop out of your head and into your body. Feel alive and present. This serves two purposes: to get you connected to your body, and to get you connected to the other women in the greatest tribe of all – *the Sisterhood.*

This book is divided into three sections. In this first section, I get raw and real, sharing my own experience of how I fell in love with being a woman and started to take care of myself.

I took a long, arduous route to write this book and I skip past some of the beginning levels of it and get right to the good stuff. My path started with wellness at the Institute for Integrative Nutrition in 2006, where I cleaned up my diet and was introduced to spirituality. I then started to explore my spirituality, which led me to quit my corporate job and become a "heart centered" entrepreneur, someone who creates a business based on helping others.

But through all the personal development to become a better business owner and "more successful," I was stepping over the most critical step: loving myself as a woman. This means understanding and trusting my feminine nature, specifically my sexuality (being in my body, owning my body, loving my body), and owning my self-worth, like really owning it. If I could summarize this it would come down to embodying the feminine trinity: self-love, self-acceptance and self-care.

You may be thinking as you read: Oh my god! I can totally relate! She is speaking my story! That is because you are me cleverly disguised as you.

Because you are the tribe, the tribe exists as a mirror reflection of you. This may sound strange because most people operate in their lives like they don't matter. "I'll just sit here to watch and listen. I'll just take it all in. I'm just a visitor today."

On the contrary. This is perhaps the most important thing for you to start to understand: you, my sister, matter the most. There is no one more important in the world than YOU. This tribe is you. How you show up is how this tribe shows up. The world is a reflection of the internal. If you want to change the world, *be* the change. Ghandi wasn't kidding!

This is where you want to really look at applying the lessons to your own life, find yourself in the conversation and show up fully at the gathering, which is really a metaphor for your life.

In the second and third sections, we're going to go deeper into the sisterhood, partnership with men and unconditionally loving our children.

But honestly, put all that aside. Put the whole concept of serving others, making a difference, changing the world aside and allow yourself to be with yourself. *You are the most important.* This book is for you to rediscover yourself. Let's begin.

Part 1: You Are the Tribe

An original poem starts each section of this book, and you are welcome to download them at SistershipCircle.com/downloads.

May the poems bring you closer to truth and light in your own journey.

I Am a New Generation Feminine Leader
I am a new generation feminine leader
And that's my truth.
My truth fully self-expressed is most important.
My truth is that I am a conduit and co-create with the divine.
I am an instrument to be used by Spirit to create love in the world
through vulnerability, connection and presence.
My truth is that we are all connected and all that keeps us
separate is the ego's voice saying, "I am special."
My truth is that all are welcome.
Leave no one behind. Leave nothing behind.
There is nothing to hide or avoid. All aspects of ourselves
are beautiful.
My truth is harmony, integration, and unity.
My truth is whole, full, and complete.
My truth is free; I hold nothing back, allowing it to come
up and through.
My truth is universal in the personal.
My truth is ME inside of WE.
My truth is all that is light and dark.
My truth is my soul expressed through form.
My truth is simply to BE.

Chapter 1: Embody the Feminine

"I cultivate my inner wisdom and feminine super powers through listening to myself."

You've found this book because you want to change the world. You want to make a difference. You want to make your life count. You know you were brought here to "do good" in the world and I'm going to tell you how you can do it.

Lean in closely. I really want you to get this. **It starts with your putting yourself first.** That's right, you are the Queen Bee. Numero Uno. The fairest of them all.

And because you are the most important, the only one out there, the powerful creator, it's time for you to fully own the truth of who you are *as a woman in flesh and blood.*

Women … we have the power to create, the ability to birth. We go through enormous pain to bring babies into this world, and that's not all we are capable of. The power to create. Creativity. Magic. Miracles.

You have forgotten who you are as a woman. That's all right. Most women have. Most women have taken on the role of acting like men, trying to prove themselves as worthy by achieving more, climbing the corporate ladder, gaining prestige, doing it all.

It's a bunch of bullshit. It's not the natural expression of who we are. (I'm giving you fair warning now that I may get really fired up and start swearing in this book, and that's me really owning my freedom to speak up, to get loud, to use my voice. If it bothers you, look within at what belief you've bought into that says that it is indecent for a woman to use profanity).

The truth is, I'm tired of giving my power away. Marianne Williamson, author of *A Return to Love*, says western women should be a moral force on the planet, and that's me! I no longer care to please others, look good and be a good girl. I'm standing up, telling the truth as I experience it, and letting you in on a few secrets that they forgot to tell us in grade school.

The very first thing I want you to understand is that you don't have to *do* anything. Nothing. Nada. Jack diddly squat.

Nope. You don't need to work for the man or like a man. You don't even need to start your own business. You don't need to run around volunteering for this organization and that organization. You don't need to do anything … to prove your self-worth. To prove that you matter. To prove that your life is worth living.

Take a deep breath. *Breathe.* If there is one thing I want you to get from this book, it's this: **you are enough just as you are**. You are worthy simply because you were born.

Does this mean you should sit in bed all day doing nothing? If you feel like it, by all means do it! (By the way: that's not what I mean.) What I mean is that you are so powerful, so creative, so magical that all you need to do is "be." That is enough.

You know when you see a woman who looks so radiant that she is "glowing?" That woman isn't doing anything in particular; however, she is magnetic and inspiring. She has people around her buzzing with excitement, and they want to do something for her. She just continues to glow and radiate while others feel empowered to take action.

This is the power of embodying the feminine. It has nothing to do with "doing" and everything to do with "being."

It is the essence of a woman. Her beauty, her intuition, her knowing. This essence is underneath all the busyness, the doingness, the facades and the masks. It is at the core of every woman and the only thing you really need to be doing is letting go of the need to prove yourself, look good, fit in and try hard.

All you need to do is *be you*. And who you are at the core is located in your womb, the seat of your sexuality, the essence of your femininity that has been shut down, shamed and oppressed. As women we have been living from the neck up, completely disconnected from our bodies' natural ability to feel. The sensations in your body are one of the most reliable sources of information, and yet we have gone numb.

In this first section of this book, we will be looking at the different aspects of what it means to be a woman today, and how you can reclaim those parts of yourself that you have been ashamed of so you can step back into *being yourself.*

Your power comes from your connection to source (i.e., God, goddess, universe, the Divine, spirit) and your ability to channel that source from your womb.

It's pretty awe-inspiring when you think about the fact that you can create life. What a miracle you are as a woman with this ability! You've got it all within you and yet you have been operating most of your life from your head, figuring out how to do what others think you should be doing.

So it's time to connect. *To embody. To feel. To express our sensuality. To get into those lower chakras and unleash our power.*

This is what I call the *descent of the feminine*. Getting real. Getting in our bodies. Getting dirty as we stick our hands in the earth and feel.

We are at a time when we've been burned out, turned off, and completely disenfranchised within the system. The system no longer works and we want out. We know there is a better way and we're not keeping our mouths shut any longer.

So we've been remembering, reconnecting with our roots. This is where tribe comes in. There is something so appealing right now about old tribe culture where rituals and ceremonies took place. Where it took an *entire tribe to raise a child*.

We've been searching the history books for what worked and what has been hidden, purposely, from our view. We're rediscovering how much has been taken away to keep us obedient and docile workers of the system.

But you, my sister, are the Queen Bee. And where did the Queen Bees hang out in ancient culture? In a circle of High Priestesses, serving a higher purpose.

Introducing the High Priestess

The High Priestess represents wisdom, serenity, knowledge and understanding. She is often described as the guardian of the unconscious. She sits in front of the thin veil of awareness, which is all that separates us from our inner selves. The High Priestess knows the secret of how to access these realms. She represents spiritual enlightenment and inner illumination, divine knowledge and wisdom. She has a deep, intuitive understanding of the Universe and uses this knowledge to teach rather than to try to control others. She reminds you to listen to and trust your inner voice.

For the male, he must learn of his 'anima' or female side, or he will fail to grow. For a woman, the High Priestess suggests that she must learn to trust herself and to be truly feminine, rather than succumbing to the pressures of having to act more like her male counterparts.

~ *From Biddy Tarot* [5]

Back in the Ancient Egyptian days, women who were married to priests would work within the temples. In the old and Middle Kingdoms (2050 to 1650 B.C.E) the women priests were usually involved in the Hathor cult, with Hathor being the god of fertility. A priestess was in charge of managing the god's affairs and some of the high priestesses were women. Other female goddesses such as Neith and Pakhet were served by female priests.

One of the most popular Egyptian high priestesses is Isis, the goddess and queen of fertility, the archetype for creation. The myth of Isis represents our feminine attributes – intuition, psychic abilities, love, compassion, yin energies, mother nurturer, the high priestess, the metaphoric goddess in all creation myths. She is the essence of the feminine energy, which is part of us all.

MORE ABOUT ISIS:

Isis is a goddess in Ancient Egyptian religious beliefs whose worship spread throughout the Greco-Roman world. She was worshipped as the ideal mother and wife as well as the patroness of nature and magic. She was the friend of slaves, sinners, artisans and the downtrodden, but she also listened to the prayers of the wealthy, maidens, aristocrats, and rulers. Isis is often depicted as the mother of Horus, the hawk-headed god of war and protection (although in some traditions Horus's mother was Hathor). Isis is also known as protector of the dead and goddess of children.

The name Isis means "Throne." Her headdress is a throne. As the personification of the throne, she was an important representation of the pharaoh's power. The pharaoh was depicted as her child, who sat on the throne she provided.

The high priestess is often depicted in the Tarot card deck, as quoted in the beginning of this chapter. What does she represent to us and what can we learn from this ancient archetype?

First of all, we can take these ancient myths and apply them to our own modern lives. The high priestess is a woman who devotes herself to something higher than herself. She gives her life in service to the divine. She is the bridge between God and earth. She is a leader, a visionary, someone who sees beyond.

She is not separate from you. She is a part of you. She is you.

Your Feminine Qualities

In school and society, we have been taught to be masculine. Why? Because we are taught male norms and lessons that favor the male perspective.

Do the following qualities sound familiar? These are things you are taught to cultivate to be a better and more productive citizen of the world.

Freedom	Focus	Passion	Confidence
Direction	Integrity	Independence	Awareness
Logic	Stability	Discipline	Authenticity

These are great qualities, right? There is nothing wrong with them; in fact, they are wonderful for getting things done, producing results and being successful in the world. No doubt, developing these qualities has gotten me to where I am today.

Yet they are only half of what makes us human. They are imbalanced when cultivated alone without paying attention to what comes naturally and instinctively to us as women.

Now take a look at the feminine qualities and rate yourself on a scale of 1 to 10, 1 being non-existent in your life to 10 being a superpower of yours:

___ Intuition
___ Feelings
___ Compassion
___ Connection
___ Nurturing
___ Receptivity
___ Sensitivity
___ Softness
___ Gentleness
___ Sensuality
___ Surrender
___ Patience
___ Inclusion
___ Honoring of process
___ Complementary
___ Cooperative
___ Diffused
___ Relational
___ Forgiveness
___ Introspection
___ Healer
___ Empowerment–empowering and empowered

Your Mystical Powers

What it means to be a woman includes more than feminine and masculine qualities. We are blessed with mystical powers, too. Women are naturally empathic, which means we have the ability to understand and share the feelings of another. Being an "empath" means being aware of and sensing your surroundings – whether positive or negative. You can literally pick up the feelings and emotions of others.

You, as a woman, have special gifts, depending on which sense (seeing, hearing, feeling, smelling, tasting, touching) is stronger for you and how sensitive you are to outside energy.

These special gifts are called the CLAIR SENSES. Clair Senses in psychic terms are translated: clairvoyance, clairaudience, clairsentience, clairscent, clairtangency, and clairgustance. Additional gifts are clairempathy and channeling.

✻⁓❨✤❩ᘿ✻

How many times have you had déjà vu, feeling like you've heard or seen something before? Or you just had that feeling that something was going to happen.

Society has deemed these so-called psychic abilities a farce, and this was a control tactic to have people obey the higher authorities. When they burned witches, it was a fight between the pagans and the church. It's time, women, that we claim our powers back. Start thinking and feeling for yourself. Start trusting yourself and all of your preceding generations of feminine embodied knowledge.

As a spiritual seeker, I have always wanted the truth. I have been on a quest for the truth ever since my mom yanked my brother and me out of Sunday school when I was around twelve years old. She wanted us to find our own God.

I became very interested in the teachings of Buddhism, but had no desire to be a Buddhist or follow any religion for that matter. When I heard about a non-denominational meditation practice that was the original teaching from Gautama the Buddha when he sat under the Bodhi tree over 2500 years ago, I had to do it.

The first time I did Vipassana, which is ten days of silent meditation with up to eleven hours of sitting practice a day, I was shocked by how much I could feel. It felt like electric currents running in my body. I became so sensitive! My dreams were weird and uncanny ... I woke up at two in the morning from a bad dream in which an event where I was scheduled to speak was cancelled. That same week, the event actually was cancelled. It was through this experience that I came to the conclusion that everyone has psychic abilities. We have just numbed ourselves from experiencing them and have not been taught how to hone them.

Throughout this journey, as you begin to tap into the feminine, slowing down and allowing yourself to be, you will notice yourself becoming more creative and even more psychic. The busyness of everyday life keeps you distracted from tapping into your mystical power. The silence and stillness allows you to be more magnetic and provides the place where magic and miracles appear.

Keep these CLAIR SENSES in mind as you go through your journey. This is not something to figure out, but something you will just start to know over time.

You'll notice that I am not giving you a "how to" to figure out in your head. This embodied practice requires you to learn to trust your feelings and intuition and to trust the wise woman who speaks to you through your body.

Clairvoyant (clear vision) – Do you see images? Visions?

Clairaudience (clear audio /hearing) – Do you hear voices other than your own? Do words come to you seemingly out of nowhere?

Clairsentience (clear sensation or feeling) – Do you have a knowing feeling in your stomach?

Clairempathy (clear emotion) – Can you feel what others are feeling?

Stepping into the High Priestess for your life and for the world starts with developing your feminine super powers, including your clair senses.

Yes, you are spiritual.
Yes, you are special.
Yes, you are intuitive.
Yes, you are even psychic.
Yes, you have super powers.
Yes, you don't have to work so hard.
Yes, you can just BE.

While the mind may be thinking, this is a bunch of woo-woo fluff, there is a part of you down in your womb that *knows* what I am talking about.

Trust yourself. To trust yourself you must begin to open yourself up to become a conduit for the divine to flow through you. Allow yourself to be a riverbed where the power of source comes through you as your very own super powers. Learn to channel your superpowers to be a source of connection with women and inspiration for men. Once you start to trust yourself, you can start to trust others.

Trust comes from within. It is a choice to be open to learn new things, receptive to your inner guidance and willing to speak your truth.

When I've told the truth about my feelings, I've felt more connected.

When I've told the truth about the lies I told in the past, I've been forgiven.

When I've told the truth about my resistance, I've opened up doors for freedom.

When I've told the truth about my fears, I've broken through my glass ceiling.

Truth telling and vulnerability are key elements to a new type of tribe that has been emerging, one that transcends all others through the connection of the human heart and soul. This tribe I'm talking about, where women gather in circle to love and support one another in the most authentic way possible, heals the "I'm not good enough" belief through vulnerable and intimate sharing. You can apply these lessons to any group to help it go deeper in service to the members.

You are not reading this as an outside observer. Instead, you are actually stepping into an experience. By the end of this book, my intention is that you feel your own strength and power as a woman. You open your heart and fall in love with yourself being a woman. You stop being so hard on yourself and forgive yourself. Through forgiveness you integrate the shadow parts of yourself. Through integration you accept your life as it is. Through acceptance you become a spiritual adult and no longer operate from the belief that "you are not enough."

Most people are not acting as adults; they are acting as little children looking for unconditional love.

Imagine if millions of women stepped into this container and had the experience of unconditionally loving, accepting and caring for themselves. Imagine if millions of women took on this lifestyle practice of embodying the High Priestess, cooperating with other women in sisterhood, inspiring and empowering men, and coming into harmony with the natural cycles and rhythms of the earth. This is what's possible when women gather with one another as a real, authentic tribe.

Embodiment

For years, I learned in a very masculine way. I learned how to create structures and take action. I learned how to think, problem- solve, and analyze.

I had many a-ha's. I became very smart and intelligent. I knew transformation, but I was still sick, unhappy and restless. I was agitated.

Transformation does not come from books or lectures. The a-ha's can occur, true, but awareness does not equal change. If you think about the caterpillar transforming into a butterfly, it is a physical metamorphosis, an embodied experience. Something physically changes in the body.

In this book, I will take you through my own journey, and give you practices that you can apply along the way.

It's up to you to take the embodied action. Your transformation is up to you. I cannot give it to you. No one can. I do not profess to be a guru and give you the answers. I will step into the High Priestess and create the container with rituals for you to step into your High Priestess. *It's up to you.*

It's really not about one archetype or one facet of being a woman. It's about embodying ALL of it. Playing the full range. As a woman, you are complex, mysterious and deep. Find your strengths and the archetypes that really call to you, and start to explore the other ones.

Now that you know more about embodying the feminine, let's go deeper. There are four ways to participate.

1. Read the book as if you were sitting down with me for a cup of tea. This is a perfect place to start. Allow yourself to soak it up. Listen intently. Practice being present.

2. See how this material applies to your own life. Take a few moments to answer the journaling questions at the end of each chapter.

3. Go deeper and play full out. Treat this book as a map and chart your own journey. Go to http://SistershipCircle.com/Playbook and download the PlayBook.

4. Take the journey with your sisters for accountability and support. Start a local sister circle using The How to Lead Circle eBook. Go to http://SistershipCircle.com/ebook.

Fear may be arising … *I'll stick with Number 1 and that way I won't have to over-commit to anything and potentially fail.* I invite you to look a little deeper with me right now. We seek for answers out there. We want someone to give us all the answers. We ask people to fix and heal us.

Number 2 through 4 are about stepping into being the High Priestess of your own life. Creating your own rules. Starting to think, feel and act for yourself. Claiming your power. Playing full out. Owning it. Taking power into your own hands.

Stepping into the High Priestess is scary because so many of us were burned at the stake as witches hundreds of years ago. Fear, guilt, shame and competition have been implanted in us.

We've been conditioned to follow the herd, to take someone else's word as Truth. This is simply my journey, not the ultimate Truth. That's for you to discover for yourself through your own experience. If anything, I want you to walk away inspired and empowered to stand for yourself. To trust yourself. To know yourself. To be YOU and you only.

There is no "right" way to do this. You can't possibly fail. The rewards are much greater for those who are willing to go for it and take a risk.

The magic we hold as women exists as our Inner Wisdom and our Sense Perception. The "work" is not masculine. It is not about doing something for accomplishment. I'm not loading you with a bunch of tasks. The "work" is feminine. Listening, reflecting, connecting, breathing, loving, feeling. Learning how to simply BE.

Sister Spotlight: Katherine's Story

I was convinced I was balanced. I already had a strong feminine side. I could dance in front of a crowded room and evoke a dripping sensuality that would give your grandfather a boner (without Viagra). I was also working 4 jobs to pay for my own business and had convinced myself I was "in flow." I had graduated first in my class from naturopathic medical school, but somehow still felt a deep sense of inadequacy. If I had it so together, why was I so miserable?

When I joined Sistership Circle, the thought of one more commitment contracted my body so thoroughly I was sure I would burst. In fact, I did burst and it was exactly what I needed. Within the first night of Sistership Circle I came to a profound realization. I had been delusional. Everything I had done up to this point in my life had been to prove my worth, to earn approval from others, and to feel like I deserved to be on this planet. I belly danced to prove I was sexy and desirable. I became a doctor because I needed a title to prove I was smart. I started my own business to prove I could do it all on my own. My achievements weren't solely seeded by inadequacy. I had good intentions behind my endeavors as well. I genuinely did enjoy the expression of dance and did really want to help people as a doctor, but my experience was tainted with a need for validation. I was pushing so hard, and none of it ever felt like enough. I didn't feel like enough.

I had seen it in my patients too. Women pushing themselves so hard...for what? So much pushing, resulting in adrenal fatigue, thyroid conditions, and even infertility. If we reject our feminine through stuffing our emotions and constantly pushing our bodies and minds, our bodies may take away the most defining characteristic of our womanhood, the ability to conceive and birth a child. Our feminine bodies aren't designed to run like a man. Our biochemistry and physiology are different. A symphony of hormones is initiated based on our mental and emotional experiences. Stress and emotions have a very real effect on our physical bodies. I have seen women embrace their feminine, embody their feminine, and change the course of their health.

Through Sistership Circle I had a safe place to identify my wounds and reintegrate the parts of myself I had rejected. To embody the feminine, I had to identify the parts of the feminine I had cut off.

To heal yourself as a woman, you must embrace all facets of the feminine and all facets of YOU, especially the dark, scary parts.

I am incredibly grateful to have had the support of my sisters while embracing my darkness, the sadness, the jealousy, the resentment, the anger, the despair. I had to embody these qualities that I had judged as "evil". As I embraced each one, its hold on me lessened.

Sistership Circle held me as I spent weeks in tears because my body and soul demanded it. When I say weeks, I mean hours a day, everyday, for weeks. I almost quit everything to move back in with my parents, in Chicago, in January. Yes, that's how bad it was. I remember Tanya sharing with me that the healing way of the feminine is through the descent, the darkness, that the only way out is through. I surrendered. I not only gave into the tears and despair, I gave up the guilt of not being productive.

During this process I learned to trust myself, to trust my experience, to trust what my body needed regardless of my schedule. Years of providing the "right" answers to parents, teachers, and partners had me distanced from my truth and it took radical acceptance of all of me to feel that my worth isn't dependent on achievements or approval. A funny thing happens when you welcome your darker side into your heart: your light gets brighter. Once you've illuminated the dark spots, your radiance expands. You begin to recognize your wholeness, your divinity. Your beingness shifts. My beingness shifted.

Sistership Circle inspired me to go even deeper with the work and trust my gut enough to do Explosive Sexual Healing. These two programs allowed me to shift my beingness to such a degree that I was able to quit multiple jobs, hire a team, and refocus my medical practice on holistic fertility, a mission that fulfills my heart by combining natural medicine, belly dance, sexuality, emotional healing and so much more. It is a mission that fulfills by my heart by supporting women reclaiming their feminine power and bodies in the most natural act of creation in the world. Even the business structure reflects femininity. As a team, we co-create the meetings and utilize ritual regularly, invoking our priestesses. Once I surrendered to my heart, to my worth, to my creation being important because I say so, life became so much more fun.

I recreated myself and recreated my business. I create in the world because I feel moved, because it is fun and exciting, because serving others brings me joy, because as a woman it is my goddess given right to create. I still dance, but I dance for me. I'm still a doctor, but I don't need the title. I'm still a business owner, but I do it my way. And when I feel the bitterness creep in, I take time to honor it. I take time to go into the darkness. Embodying the feminine means embodying all of her. Embodying the feminine means being all of her. Embodying the feminine means being all of YOU.

~ Dr. Katherine M. Zagone, ND

Inquiry Journaling/Affirming Rituals

Answer these questions in your journal:

What is most beautiful to me about the feminine?
What is most scary to me about the feminine?
What negative stories did I hear about the feminine . . .

From mother?
    From father?
    From friends?
    From school?
    From other family members?

Ready to go deeper?

Go to http://SistershipCircle.com/Playbook to download your free PlayBook.

Chapter 2: Open Your Heart to Receive

"I am willing and open to receive divine guidance, love and support."

I have nothing to hide. Nothing to be ashamed of. I am a woman. And what it means to be a woman is to be …

Fierce. Soft. Sexy. Bitchy. Sweet. Vulnerable. Direct. Nurturing. Compassionate. Uncompromising. Angry. Protective. Regal. Embodied. Expressed. Outspoken. Listening. Loving. Mother. Queen. Sister.

I stand here half-clothed, knowing I am attracting attention, catcalls and judgments, stares and gasps.

But this is all of me. All parts. And I will not cover up because it overwhelms you with passion, desire and lust. I will not cover up because it embarrasses you and makes you uncomfortable. I will not cover up because society deems it inappropriate and sinful. I will not cover up because you are jealous and insecure in your own sexuality.

I will not cover up. I will not stifle my self-expression. I will not. What I will do is keep my head up. I will strip down to the essence of who I am. I will bare it all.

Years of shame. Years of feeling used. Years of wondering if you only liked me for my body and not my brains. Years of closing my heart to you in fear of getting hurt. Years of mistrust. Peeled off of me. Shed. Stripped away.

I looked within. I changed my perspective. I started to trust myself. I claimed my self-worth. And I fell in love with me. All of me. There is nothing wrong with me. I am perfect just the way I am.

I am sexy, beautiful, hot and drop dead gorgeous.

I am a bitch who asserts her boundaries and doesn't tolerate manipulation. I am compassionate, loving, sweet and vulnerable.

I am human and make mistakes.

I will not compromise any part of myself to please you, and I give you permission to claim all parts of yourself as well. When we can truly see, hear and value each other for who we are — all parts — we will create a new world. Free.

Free from judgment, hatred, prejudice and discrimination.
Free from loneliness, disconnection, and unworthiness.
Free from the confines of our own minds.
Free to express our essence.
Free to love unconditionally.
Free.

Trust yourself and say YES to all of it. For me to get to this place of embodying the High Priestess, I had to be willing to take off my mask, open my heart and receive the guidance that was coming through.

And the guidance was to go deep into the dark. I had to go through the dark night of the soul. What is the dark night of the soul? It's when we face the shadow side of ourselves, the part that we hide in shame and we don't want to see or be seen. It feels evil, dark, scary and ugly.

It *was* scary. I felt like I was being stripped bare, ripped apart, and cracked open. But before I go there in my story, this chapter is about setting an intention. *That intention is to be willing and open to receive.*

As nurturers, we are so good at giving. We take care of others, most of the time at the expense of our own sanity and wellbeing.

- How often have you felt resentful of the people you give to?
- How many times have you wished you said NO to someone to say YES to yourself?
- How many times have you sacrificed yourself in the name of "service?"

It's a distraction. It's coming from "not enough." It's a way of feeling worthy, to feel like you matter, when really, you ARE already worthy and you already matter simply because you were born.

Only if I give will I be noticed.

Only if I serve will I feel my life matters.

Only if I go out of my way will I receive recognition for my hard work.

Only if I work hard will I feel a sense of fulfillment and accomplishment.

Bullshit. You have been giving it all away, sacrificing your health, depleting your energy, and dimming your light. You are not serving anyone if you are not taking care of yourself. It is time you learn a new way – through allowing and receiving.

To give in the way of the self-sacrificing martyr is an old story that we have been led to believe is the holy and good way. To give in this way is forcing and pushing from a place of "not enough" to feel worthy, abundant and special. Instead, it is coming from fear and scarcity that if you do nothing, *you will not survive.*

I have found the opposite to be true. When we are willing and open to do absolutely nothing, we get to the brink of what feels like death and then we are reborn. We finally understand that all there is to do is BE.

You are majestic in your beauty and grace. You know that your presence is enough. You know that you inspire others by sitting in your regalness, smiling. You are magnetic and don't have to say a word.

You inspire people to want to provide and protect you when you learn to receive. Deep down you know your worth, and it's time to own it.

As I said, I took the long, hard, arduous route to learn this lesson.

Resistance

When you are resistant, you are not open to the opportunities that come your way. You are closed off, stubborn, thinking you know everything, afraid of what will happen if you lost control.

Here's the progression of events when you are resistant. First you get a little tap on the shoulder. If you ignore it, you get shoved from behind. If you continue to ignore it, you get knocked over. If you still don't get it, you'll end up in the hospital. And then dead.

This is why cancer or a heart attack is such a wakeup call.

This is what Jill Bolte Taylor, a Harvard-trained brain scientist, described to Oprah Winfrey about her massive stroke at age thirty-seven. Jill listened to the miracle.

We have been taught to think that these accidents or severe circumstances are bad. But they are not. There is no right or wrong. There is nothing to fix and change. Can you go with the flow? Can you see the beautiful life-altering lesson that these circumstances really are? There are no accidents or coincidences. Everything happens for a reason.

My Story

I had everything I could have ever wanted. Or so I thought, according to the American Dream. I lived in a big house. My mom didn't work. We had two luxury cars. My mom drove me and my friends everywhere. I could play any sport I chose. Money was never an issue. I went to a good school.

How come I had everything so easy and yet everyone out there in the world suffered? Life, out there, was not easy. It was hard. And my dad worked hard to give us what we had.

My mom reminded me of it constantly. "Be grateful. Your dad works hard so we can have this life."

Instead of feeling grateful, I felt guilty. I had to work hard. I had to earn my keep. I had to do whatever it took to prove I deserved what I had. Nothing comes for free. Nothing comes to you simply because you exist. You must be a good, hard-working person.

So I worked hard to prove my worth. I got straight A's and was competitive at sports. At twelve years old, I worked at my dad's dental office doing filing (hated it!) to pay off what I felt I owed him. I had my first minimum wage job at sixteen and worked twenty-five to thirty hours a week during college.

I didn't want others to think they were less than me, that I wasn't earning my place in the world. I burned out. This pressure built up over time and I crashed. Hard.

In 2012 I lost everything. Everything I had "worked for" seemed as if it was taken from me. Stripped. Naked. All that was left was *me*. Is this enough? Am I enough with nothing left?

It started with the breakup of my boyfriend. July 28, 2011, I woke up thinking something needed to change. Maybe I would move out to take some space. I felt reliant on him.

I had a sequence of calls that morning that left me irritated. At noon, I had my Blogtalkradio show and my guest was an EFT practitioner.

[EFT means Emotional Freedom Technique, also known as "Tapping" which helps you dissipate any tension in the body.] She asked me if I would be willing to use a current example in my life to practice the technique for the listeners.

The only thing on my mind was my boyfriend and how angry and irritated I was at him. So of course, the truth teller that I am, I volunteered this information. She took me from a level ten of anger down to about a three.

He had said a few days earlier that "I was too angry and too masculine" for him. At 5:00 pm, he came home. I was lying on the bed and when he walked in, my heart started beating really fast. My stomach dropped. He sat down on the edge of the bed and looked at me.

"I think this is the end of our journey together." He had tears in his eyes and so did I. I felt sick.

At that point, I knew I had to leave. I stormed out of the house, grabbing a bag of clothes and my pillow. I sat in the car, crying hysterically. I had nowhere to go. I sat there crying for an hour.

I had my circle at 7:00 pm so that seemed like the logical place to go. I didn't want to go to my parents' house. I showed up at the meeting, still bawling like a baby. The women held me and massaged me and listened to me. After about fifteen minutes of crying, I said I was ready to talk about our dreams. I slept there at the house in the living room. Again, avoiding and resisting. Not remembering that I had woke up that same morning thinking something needed to change.

For the next few months, I went from friend's house to parents' house to Vipassana meditation to parents' house. I felt broken. Depressed. Unsure of myself.

Who was I now that I wasn't in this relationship? While it didn't define me, it was a security blanket. I felt safe. And now I was pissed that I no longer had that comfort. I felt like my foundation was ripped out from underneath me. I wasn't quite sure how I would survive on my own, so I relied on my parents.

Resistance.

I made the excuse that I needed someone to take care of me while I worked. I wanted my mom to cook and clean for me. I wanted the comfort of my parents' home, the TV, the plush couches.

I packed all my stuff up and put it in storage. I lived out of a suitcase. I went from one security blanket to another. I honestly didn't think I could survive on my own.

I didn't think I could do it. I didn't feel like I was enough. I worked my ass off for my organization formerly known as Tribal Truth, but I didn't think I deserved getting paid enough to get my own place and be self-sufficient.

I lied and told myself that I now had freedom with my stuff in storage and no rent to pay. So I bought a ticket to India for a six-week stay and took off on December 28.

Resistance.

Everything crashed. My tribe leaders left. I had no money. I owed money and I was pissed that I had to keep paying a debt when I didn't have any income. I was angry. And I still avoided, having this "wonderful time" in India. Inside I was still crying. I had this low-grade anxiety that penetrated underneath the surface. I had this edge, this tension that people could feel. I was short-tempered and irritated.

When I returned to San Diego in February, I launched into producing mode. Again avoiding and distracting myself. I booked the world tour to bring tribes to life in Vegas, London, New York, and Washington DC and reinvigorate the San Francisco area.

Resistance.

I remained angry and used my masculine energy to make it happen, despite it not quite working out the way I wanted.

I lost my cell phone in London. Washington, DC didn't happen. New York was a flop. I totaled my dream car that I just manifested a few weeks earlier while driving up to San Francisco.

With a mounting debt, I continued to drive forward to make things happen. I was going to push and push because I was determined not to fail. I was too proud to admit that my foundation was cracked and unstable.

The fear and anxiety out there is caused from the scarcity mentality within that stems from "I am not enough."

❦

"No matter what I do, it's not enough." This was running the show in early 2012. I felt broken and unworthy and uncertain.

The turning point happened in August on my way to Burning Man. We had new tribe leaders on the call. I ran our leadership calls from a very masculine place: numbers, goals, actions, plans.

Set your goal and make the numbers. Period.

I wasn't getting my way and felt frustrated on that call right before I drove in toward Black Rock City. I remember being on my phone in the bathroom at a gas station, completely frustrated with one of the leaders as she refused to set her goals.

This just wasn't working for me. How could I build this organization if no one would be accountable for anything?

After Burning Man, I drove to Las Vegas and then to Bhakti Fest. I crashed. The Desert Adventure burned me through and through. On the next call, I showed up and felt different. I felt … raw. I shared vulnerably about my pain. For some reason that morning, I just couldn't lead from that strong place anymore. So I cried and shared my fears and my "weaknesses" and for the first time, some of the leaders said they felt the most connected with me. They felt relieved that I wasn't super woman. They could relate to me. They could let down their guard and open up.

I continued to come to each call after that sharing my pain and frustration. It became my safe haven to be vulnerable. And the pain continued to pour out of me. I broke open and started to let go, unraveling, spinning out of control. Every morning, I woke up with anxiety. My heart racing, my chest tense. I had to leave my bed and immediately go to one of the hiking trails by the house.

If I showed up on the call being "masculine," the women would call me out. They just wouldn't tolerate it. They would drop me right back into that vulnerable place. I felt so emotionally raw and out of control. I felt like the business would fail at any moment. I was holding on for dear life, not wanting to trust that I was supported.

Tumbling down the rabbit hole. Nothing left to hold onto. *I was being forced to learn how to receive guidance, contribution and support.* I was being forced to crack open. And I continued to lean in. I

MORE ABOUT BURNING MAN

Burning Man is an annual event and a thriving year-round culture. The event takes place the week leading up to and including Labor Day, in Nevada's Black Rock Desert. The Burning Man organization (Black Rock City LLC) creates the infrastructure of Black Rock City, wherein attendees (or "participants") dedicate themselves to the spirit of community, art, self-expression, and self-reliance. They depart one week later, leaving no trace. As simple as this may seem, trying to explain what Burning Man is to someone who has never been to the event is a bit like trying to explain what a particular color looks like to someone who is blind. To truly understand this event, one must participate.

What started out as a small event with 20 people on San Francisco's Baker Beach in 1986 and then migrated to the Black Rock Desert has now morphed into a vibrant global year-round culture of like-minded individuals who seek to live their lives in a more meaningful, powerful and self-expressed way. Over 60,000 people attended in 2013. The Ten Principles are a reflection of the community's ethos and culture as it has organically developed since the event's inception.

wrote this blog post on October 22, after an intense conversation with two of my tribe leaders.

I started to see the lies I had told myself, the false illusion of myself. I started to see what was really going on. The truth was beginning to be illuminated.

My deep core wound

Posted by Tanya Lynn on Tuesday, October 23rd 2012

Since I was a little girl, I haven't felt like I belong. I felt judged and blamed for things that I did. I felt like whatever I did was wrong, not good enough.

Memory: I must have been in first or second grade. It was a slumber party. We were horse playing on the sleeping bags that were laid out all over the floor. One of the girls had just gotten stitches above her eye. I tripped her; she slipped on the sleeping bag, and hurt herself again. I was deeply embarrassed, felt guilt and shame. I was yelled at by an adult and felt ostracized from the group in that moment. I really didn't mean to hurt her. And yet I was in trouble. I had these types of incidences happen many times in elementary school, and I internalized them.

I felt alone. I never felt the sense of safety in community. Even being on sports teams, Girl Scouts, the popular group at school — all types of tribes — I felt like no one really had my back. At any moment, someone would turn against me. Over and over again, I struggled to speak about my feelings to my friends and family. I didn't have access to speaking my truth.

This is one reason why I created Tribal Truth. Not because I was an expert and knew what community looked like. But because I so badly wanted to be in a safe, nurturing community that I had never experienced before. I wanted women to have my back. I thought: if I build it, they'll have to have my back. They'll have to like me. They'll have to be grateful. It was a manipulative, controlling desire with a deep attachment to fix the past.

This was my "heart strategy." My heart wanted love, connection, intimacy, friendship, trust, compassion, gratitude. I had a very good strategy to get what I wanted. It comes from "I always get what I want."

I've been a very good salesperson to have others get on board with my strategy. I've been selling people on my dream to have sisterhood and tribe.

The problem is it came from a place of scarcity. I was fixing, controlling, manipulating. So the whole time, I've been struggling with: why does Tribal Truth feel so inauthentic to me? Why do I feel like we are unable to go deep? Why does it feel like people aren't really committed?

Because we feel energy. People felt the underlying inauthenticity. No one could put their finger on it, not even myself. This strategy has been an unconscious one. It has been hidden from my view. A blind spot. And yet it's hard to go really deep into truth telling when the leader is unable to do the deepest level of truth telling. The tribe is a mirror of me. So wherever I am, the tribe will reflect that.

The thing is, I've been using this strategy since I was a little kid. I was always popular, building up other kids to become popular, growing the popular crowd. Community building using my "heart strategy" has been ingrained in me since elementary school.

Last Friday, I discovered the flip side of my heart strategy: I don't really believe that the love and connection my heart desires is really possible. "No one can really go deep with me." Coming from this place of inauthenticity, of course the old patterns will continue to repeat to prove that I'm right about my story (that love and connection are not really possible).

The chaos ensues: mistrust, back stabbing, gossip, judgment, cattiness. Women join the tribe expecting everything to magically be fixed and ask, "Why isn't the tribe behind my dream like you promised?" As if showing up, the tribe will just naturally promote your business, be your friend, give you coaching and support, etc. No coincidence that this repeats. This was my strategy, my expectation: the tribe would just naturally have my back, help me with my dream, be my friends, etc.

So to keep myself safe and protected, I created my "head strategy."

Push them away, sabotage the relationship; kill them off before they can hurt me.

And the closer you try to get, the harder I am going to push back. I'm going to pull out my sticks and knives along with my shield of anger to keep you away. I will do whatever it takes. And only if you then can still survive will I consider you my friend. Only then, can I truly trust you, rely on you, believe that you have my back. So really, you can never win with me. You feel like you are never good enough for me. You feel disconnected, unloved, unappreciated, unwanted.

This makes me so sick. My strategy is so ugly it had me bawling my eyes out for about 30 minutes on Friday as one Tribe Leader moved me through a process and another held space for me. I wanted to crawl up in a hole and never come out. If you figured out this ugly truth of mine, if you found out what my dark strategy was, I was afraid you'd never ever love me and would want to run for the hills. So I might as well throw you out first. Or push you away and get angry so you leave and I can blame you for it, again supporting my "story." I have so much guilt and shame around this. And I've been using it for over 20 years.

I see how this has played out in my life over and over again. How I have done this to sabotage my closest friends and tribes that I've been a part of. As much as I want tribe, I am so scared of it. I am so afraid of getting hurt, of feeling this shame. I will build it up only to bring it down. Over and over again.

That is until now that I've discovered it and am revealing it to you. I am drawing the line in the sand.

I am asking you to be my partner: Of standing for me choosing love and abundance instead of fear and scarcity. Of standing for me to continue to go deeper into this core wound. Of standing for me to continue to love and forgive myself and allow you in.

I want you to come into my heart space. I want to connect. I really don't want to push you away. I don't want to live in accordance to my strategies anymore. I want to live free of this guilt and shame that I have been holding onto.

I know that this process I went through last week opened up a lot. And I know there is still more to discover and move through. I know that the more I open up, share, allow contribution, keep looking at myself in the mirror, keep going deeper underneath my anger, fear and frustrations, the more I forgive myself, have compassion for myself, love myself — this is the way through to the light.

This had to come up. This ugliness had to surface. I had to be with it, really feel it and access it in my body. There is nothing wrong with me. I am doing the best I can with what I have. I am imperfect. I make a ton of mistakes. It is all ok. I am ok. I am good.

I share this with you so that you can call me out on my strategy and remind me of my commitment to real community, raw truth and love.

I also share this with you because it has had an impact on you, whether directly or indirectly. You've been in my tribe and had to experience the dark energy from me in some shape or form. It may have mirrored in some way in your life. It may have shown up in your tribe. It may have left you feeling like you want to run as far away as possible from me.

I also share this with you so that we can continue to clear this out of the space, out of the tribe and create new possibilities.

While the LA Gathering a few Saturdays ago was AMAZING, I realized something that was missing: I called it "a wobbly container" which in other words meant that the integrity was out. Integrity to me is being whole and complete. I was far from whole and complete.

Integrity will continue to go out over and over again. We are imperfect and will continue to make mistakes. The lesson is in how quickly we can identify it and make ourselves whole and complete again, for the moment, until it goes back out again.

This is what I see my job is as the CEO of Tribal Truth. To keep putting my integrity back in, getting back to being whole. Integrated, connected, full, abundant, love.

I am choosing my heart's desire to be love and feel connected. I want ease and grace in intimacy. I want to let go of my shield of anger and continue to look underneath it.

I really struggled to post this because I was afraid you'd run for the hills and think "this tribe is NOT for me!" I am being with the fear and doing it anyway. You are my tribe. You deserve to know all parts of me and my experience that led you here to Tribal Truth. I am trusting that whatever your reaction is, it's perfect.

Thank you for reading this. I appreciate you.
Tanya

I've mentioned a few times my "masculine energy." It was at this time that I started to differentiate the masculine from the feminine and realize this inner turmoil within me. I saw that this conflict – the butting of heads between my inner masculine and inner feminine – was exactly what was going on out there in the world.

The masculine protector and provider. The masculine producer. The masculine warrior. My masculine served me well. It produced results. It drove my business forward. It took action. It pushed when I needed it to. It focused on an outcome and made it happen.

I really trusted my inner masculine. It was reliable. It was disciplined. It was well trained like a samurai warrior. It kept me safe. It accomplished goals and brought me success. It was controlled. Put together. Contained.

But I was exhausted. Burned out. Fatigued. And like a bottomless pit, no matter how many lives I touched, how many people I served, how many accomplishments, I never felt fulfilled. Unsatisfied. Empty. Thirsty for more. It never felt like it was enough.

When I declared I would take Tribal Truth international and launched in London, pushing to make it happen, I didn't recognize the success. Instead, I thought: that's only one city internationally. It was never enough. It will never be enough. Unfulfilling. Empty. Unsatisfying.

As women, our biology doesn't physically support constantly using masculine energy. The body gets out of balance. We do not have the testosterone levels to support the masculine forcing and producing energy. So when we push past our physical capacity, our bodies start to tax the adrenals and thyroid.

Hence, the reason most Western women using their masculine energy have a thyroid condition or adrenal fatigue. We just weren't built and designed to be result-producers in that way. So why do we do it?

Our society conditioned us when we went to the workforce. The only model was the masculine way. To fit into a culture, we had to act a certain way. It started during World War I when all the men went off to war and women had to start working in the factories.

Capitalism says that we must keep making profits. This means we must keep working until we make enough widgets to sell. To power this type of system, we must keep the machine running, spinning, at the only pace we know how, the only way we've been conditioned – which is to take the most efficient actions to drive results.

I could analyze history or I could just speak from my own experience. As a little girl, I started playing sports at five. I started ballet, hated it and quit after the first day. I played soccer, hated it, but stuck with it.

My soccer coach had a military background and drilled us like we were marines. I loved him. I loved the discipline. I loved being pushed to play harder. I was afraid to slide tackle and be aggressive so I played defender. I felt jealous of the girls who played forward and made all the goals. I wanted to be in the spotlight, the invaluable player, not the replaceable one.

I started basketball in fifth grade and quit soccer when I went into middle school. My friends and I joined year-round volleyball and basketball travelling teams.

My basketball coach had one leg and just like my soccer coach, drilled us hardcore. He made us run until we threw up. We trained for the Junior Nationals tournament in Hartford, Connecticut, in seventh grade and despite all the training, lost to the girls on the East Coast who were bigger and stronger and faster.

That same sportsman mentality to push and compete to win trickled into school. I worked hard for straight As. I felt enormous pressure to perform and constantly felt stressed out.

At a young age, I was trained to be a warrior to win and succeed no matter what. My team versus your team, and *may the best win*. And my team never won. We were never the best. I felt like a failure. I felt like I wasn't enough. There was no rest. I pushed until I made it and even then, it wasn't enough. I gave it my all.

This is how our society trains us. Play sports to win. Go to school, graduate (succeed), go to the next level, graduate (succeed), all in order to do what? Get a job. Constant movement from one level to the next. One accomplishment to the next. In a very specific order that looks like this:

School = > Job = > Marriage = > Kids = > Retire = > Die

It's a linear progression, just like a video game, that doesn't take into account your passions, desires, or freedom to indulge and revel in the moment. There is no present moment really. It's constant forward-thinking, future planning and goal-oriented.

So what's the alternative? In the process of surrendering to the stripping process, I gave up my agendas, goals, and schedules. I felt out of control. I felt like I was missing appointments, emails and phone calls. Before, my life felt so put together; in this surrendering, it felt like complete chaos.

The feminine is the flow of life. It is the creative energy. It is about acceptance, receptivity, surrendering, allowing. As I became vulnerable and opened my heart, I started to become more feminine. Emotions poured out of me and I felt my heart hurting more. The difference was that *I allowed myself to feel the emotions welling up inside of me and didn't run away from them.* I felt the pain in my chest and cried instead of avoiding and changing the subject.

This swing waaaayyy over to the feminine felt really uncomfortable. The conversations I had with the women in my life felt more organic and I desperately wanted to get to the point and have them be more intentional. But more and more, I found myself ripping up the piece of paper with my agenda, getting frustrated that I wasn't achieving my goals on my calls and wasn't covering the things I thought needed priority. Instead of forcing my agenda, I let it go. I felt the frustration and then let it go. It was a whole letting go process of wanting something and not being attached to it and going with the natural flow of the universe instead of resisting it.

Sounds woo-woo and felt woo-woo, but what I found is: *the feminine is not linear.* It is circular, diffused, organic and mysterious all in one. And it always finds its way. So we could go on a tangent and stop the agenda to deal with some emotional processing, and we would always have progress. The group would be more connected. We were real and authentic. Magic happened: we started to attract what we wanted with less effort.

I found space on my calendar. I no longer cared if I slept in, went for a midday walk on the beach, spent an entire morning processing my emotions. I allowed myself to feel sad or depressed and didn't try to force myself to get back to happy.

I dismissed the pursuit of happiness altogether as bullshit. Procrastination no longer existed as a word in my vocabulary. Neither did LAZY. Everything exists in what Gay Hendricks calls Einstein Time.

Time is relative. It is infinite. I no longer found myself attached to certain timelines and timeframes. When the time was right, things would happen. And they would happen really fast because when everything is in alignment, magic happens and exactly the right resources show up to support an intention in being fulfilled.

Life is one big breath. Inhale. Exhale. Expansion. Contraction. Cyclical. Organic. Flow in. Flow out. Flow in again.

What I realized is I had to swing over to the feminine extreme because I had never been there before. I had to have a big expansion and inhale because I had been exhaling to the point of exhaustion my entire life.

Once I had enough flow, and felt filled up, it was time to contract. Instead of swinging all the way back to the other side, the masculine, I could find myself in the center.

This is the balance, the integration. When our breathing is normal, steady and rhythmic.

But life is not always level and steadfast. It is peaks and valleys, extreme opposites of dark and light. We run and sprint, bringing our breathing irregular and short, and then later we sleep, breathing long and deep.

As I started to understand and follow my own breath through Vipassana meditation, I had a new awareness of my body sensations.

I could not crave the good feeling and I could not avert from the bad feeling. There is no good and bad. There is dark and light, there is masculine and feminine, there is happy and sad, love and fear, anger and joy. Extremes. Pleasant and unpleasant but not good and bad. Both are equal, both are worthy.

As I began to embrace all parts of me and understand that my body sensations would come and go, which is a never-ending process of understanding the impermanence of life, I began to trust.

Trust that everything is going to be all right.
Trust that I am supported by an all-knowing universe.
Trust God's plan.
Trust that there is a different way of doing leadership.
Trust my feminine as much as my masculine.

There is nothing wrong with the current structure. There is actually nothing wrong with the world today. There is nothing bad about what's happening. We are experiencing darkness and chaos and it is all part of the process. We constantly operate from fear of the unknown. And ultimately, what is that? Death.

This is why we are also constantly trying to fix and change the world. Stop war. Why? Because of death. Stop heart attacks. Why? Because of death.

We must embrace the world as it is today, no matter how unpleasant it may feel. It is impermanent. It will shift and change. That is the law of nature. Remember, death leads to birth and birth leads to death. The circle of life. Look outside your window at the trees and flowers and you will see a cycle of birth and death.

Death is the most taboo subject in our culture. More so than sex and money. Why? Why do we fear this inevitable part of life? Why do we make death a "Problem?" We could look at life as "Problem/ Solution" or we can look at life as a "Dance."

There is a beginning, a middle and an end of a dance. There are no rules to dance, just getting in tune with the music, letting go of control and allowing the music to move through you.

Through this unpeeling, unmasking, stripping down process of my identity, I still held tightly onto Tribal Truth. I see now how perfect it was. I see how I still had lessons to get. Like a mother clinging to her child, I was unwilling to fully let it go.

I share with you my struggle and my painful journey into the darkness because I want you to get that you are not alone if you are in that depression, or you are afraid of going there because of what it may mean for your livelihood or your relationships.

They said that 2012 was going to be the year of the apocalypse. 12-21-12 was the end of the Mayan Calendar where structures and systems would crash and fail and the world was going to end. Instead, what I have experienced is a different kind of death. Purification. Burning through. A complete and utter LETTING GO of the old. People all around me were experiencing a profound shift in their lives from DOING to BEING. People were shedding their old identities. People were experiencing a kind of death and rebirth. This type of death is equally as scary as the physical. And it's not over. It's like layers of an onion and just when you think you have gone deep enough, there is still more there to look at and peel off.

If you have a full closet, it's hard to put new clothes in it right? There is no space for them. But if you have an empty closet, all you want to do is buy a new wardrobe. If you are holding onto so many skeletons in the closet, so to speak, you are draining your energy. Take care of yourself and in more ways than one. Your vision will become clear when it's not clouded by the past. You will be open to receive when you have let go. Trust fully. Overcome the resistance to stand fully in your power.

Imagine the high priestess:

She has her arms outstretched, heart open, ready to receive all that life has to offer and she does not back down in fear. She does not shrink back. She is soft, willing, relaxed.

She has purified herself and protects her own energy from getting drained from others.

We'll be diving deeper into purification in the next chapter.

Sister Spotlight: Patrina's Story

When managing four kids and a business as a single mother, life moves very fast and there are many balls to juggle. I am always doing and creating, nurturing and taking care of people or things. I do my best to stay in the moment because that's about as much as my mind can handle. I have healed and moved through so much since losing my husband to suicide and finding out that I was pregnant with my fourth child the same day in 2009. My heart was broken beyond repair, and I wasn't sure how I'd move forward.

In February 2013, I woke up with an inner knowing that it was time to leave Las Vegas. It was time to release all of my crutches, release the memories of life with my husband, release all of the associations with who I was, and walk away from everything I knew to discover who I'm meant to be. It was time to create my fresh start.

28 days later I packed up my four kids, sold my house and left Las Vegas where I had family, friends, and support to move to San Diego where I knew no one. My transition has been a wild and crazy and beautiful ride but it's also been a REALLY hard one - a journey that I share more about in my book "Motherhood's Not for Punks."

In just 2 short years since moving to San Diego, I went from knowing no one and having no support with my kids and my business, and not knowing how to ask for or receive help, to cultivating a beautiful community of friends and mentors. I opened myself up to the vulnerability involved with asking for and receiving support and love from others. It's been a long road, but with the help of my sisters, I came out on the other side of the struggle stronger and full of unconditional love.

The days of women being catty and in competition with each other are gone. It's an old paradigm that doesn't serve us as women. We live in an abundant Universe. There is plenty of money, men, and beauty to go around. The only way to grow stronger as women and as a community is to realize that we are all reflections of each other. It is also the only way to move humanity forward and raise incredible kids. It takes a village to raise a child. It takes a village of beautiful reflections of yourself to remind you of your strength and your beauty in the moments when you forget. Sistership Circle provides exactly that.

I joined Sistership Circle during a time when I was highly stressed, overwhelmed, and bombarded with deadlines around the completion of my book. So although I heard nothing but great things about circle, my first response was to say no. I felt super resistant and like it was not the right time. But after some thought, I realized that Sistership Circle was exactly what I needed. The whole process of writing my book and engaging the help of the community to help fund the publishing of the book was to break the cycle of feeling like I/we have to do everything alone. We don't! There are so many people waiting and wanting to support us if we would just ask.

Sistership Circle has become such an important part of my week. It has provided a sacred space where I don't have to be strong. I don't have to have all the answers or be the leader of anything. It's an opportunity to BE and FEEL whatever I want without judgment; a place to be held, supported and loved through my full range of emotion.

Your community of support will not come to you. Someone has to initiate and create it. We all have obligations and demands on our time so connection and sisterhood often gets put on the back burner, but it's important and must be prioritized higher.

I am grateful to Tanya Lynn for having the foresight to create this incredible legacy for all of the emerging feminine leaders in the world. It has been super nurturing to my soul having this group of ladies to share challenges and triumphs with. Knowing and holding the intention for each other's dreams makes celebrating the accomplishment of the dreams that much more fun!

Open your heart to receive the love and support that you deserve. Acknowledge the oneness and embrace your fellow sisters. We are all in this together. She rises, We rise!

~ Patrina Wisdom

Inquiry Journaling/Affirming Rituals

1. Where has resistance stopped you in your tracks or kept you playing small?

2. The feminine is all about the flow of life. Describe an experience of your being in divine feminine flow, a time when you felt such positive energy you could do anything!

Chapter 3: Forgive Yourself

"I fully and completely forgive myself and others."

June 12, 2013:

Dear God,

Please forgive me for not loving myself for being me, Your child.

Allow me to surrender to You and be love.

Give me the strength to have compassion and acceptance for all beings.

Give me the courage to keep doing this deep work with self-care and self-love.

Give me the reminder that I do not need to "get rid" of any part of myself, only to integrate.

I am so grateful for the abundance of love and support in my life. It is everywhere.

Thank you for always being there for me, my guiding light.

Thank you for blessing me with my gifts. Please show me the way. I give myself up to be used by you for my divine contract.

I am ready. I am willing. I am listening.

Love,
Tanya

My dear sister, thank you for being so receptive to my story. I am so grateful for you. It is because of you that I have the strength and courage to keep opening and find strength in being vulnerable.

Thank you for being you. I am present to who you are: someone who wants to live your full potential and live a life worth living. Someone who cares about others. Someone who has a dream to make a difference.

I feel our collective heart. The pain we feel when others are sad. The grief we feel when others suffer. The love we feel when someone opens her heart.

Right now, we are being called to take action on the planet, and that action is to love: daily interactions of love; phone calls, emails, Facebook posts of love; hugs; looking deeply into someone's eyes and telling them, "I love you."

To take a stand for someone is to love them deeply and practice what I call "compassionate rigor" — *speaking the truth with the understanding that their suffering is a mirror of your own.*

Loving one another begins with loving ourselves and fully accepting and loving *all* parts of ourselves. We must be kind and gentle to ourselves because we are doing the best we can with what we've learned so far on this journey, and we must not get sucked into the delusion of our stories made up from our past.

I choose love today.

When I look back at 2012, I have this insight: by going deep into review of the unfolding of my journey, I am able to see that I am tested over and over again to surrender to love.

I was able to forgive myself for everything I thought I had done wrong, for every mistake I thought I had made. And this forgiveness has given me so much space in my heart to love.

How are you feeling right now? Have you cleared out your judgments that may have accumulated? Is your heart open to love? Or are you holding back, shrinking back, constricted?

On June 21, 2013, a beautiful bright and clear morning, I went for a walk at Fletcher Cove with one of my best friends, who I call my little sister. She wrote a Forgiveness List, forgiving herself for everything she ever blamed herself for. She read the list aloud as we gazed at the ocean. As she started to cry, I cried with her. I allowed myself to feel the forgiveness within myself. I allowed it to penetrate my own heart. I felt her pain in letting go. I felt her suffering from years of blame and shame. I felt my own heart letting go.

I had a business partner when I started Tribal Truth. She was my best friend, my sister. And yet I was jealous of her. She was not afraid of taking center stage and I was, so I competed against her. Secretly. I didn't tell anyone, but I felt it. I had to prove my worth.

Slowly, we lost sight of the same vision. I felt her moving away from me energetically and I blamed her for not doing any work, even though I didn't create any space for her to be my partner. It was my way or the highway. I was right. I had to be. Because without being right, what did I have?

The only thing I knew how to do was sabotage relationships. It was my pattern: my life was divided into one- to two-year increments and then I had to change something. I couldn't maintain a relationship for more than one to two years. I couldn't maintain a job or business for more than one to two years. I couldn't live in the same home for more than one to two years.

I had an addiction to change, movement, instability. I was a wanderer, a gypsy spirit, a nomad. I wanted to uproot. I wanted to create chaos so I could save the day.

And so I asked her to leave the business at the beginning of 2011. As 50-50 owners, we settled on a price for me to buy her out of the business.

At the time, I thought I was invincible with the successful Los Angeles launch and a few more launches scheduled for the quarter. Piece of cake. I felt expanded; this was my opportunity to take flight. The opposite happened.

⁂❀⁂

After the New York and San Francisco launches, I went through another split with my romantic partner and plummeted into a dark hole. I felt alone. I was in grief and mourning. I could barely hang on to the business. I felt trapped, a slave to the debt. I had to keep on working despite feeling completely incapable.

And so I blamed her. I squirmed and writhed in pain. She held me to the agreement, which made me even more angry. I was livid. Incensed. Furious.

How could she choose money over friendship? How could she want to make me suffer like this? It felt like I was working for her. Every month.

And I resisted against it. I didn't want to make money simply because I didn't want to pay her. I would rather close the business altogether than continue to feel like a slave. I hated her. I hated myself even more for agreeing. For more than 20 months I beat myself up and blamed her for it.

Late in the afternoon of December 7, 2012, my father's birthday, I was fuming on the phone with a friend. I mean really fuming. I was screaming like a lunatic into the phone in the middle of the street in Leucadia, California.

My friend, bless her soul, just held space, listening and gently asking me to take another action. *"Can you forgive yourself? And in the process, forgive her? Can you write her a letter asking her to forgive the debt?"*

"There's no way!" I barked back.

A month earlier, another friend told me that I needed to borrow the money and pay her off by the end of 2012 so that I could move on. *"Whatever it takes, Tanya. Get on your knees and beg God to help you. Pray for a miracle."*

As I was ranting and swearing in the street, I remembered that conversation. I got quiet. When I got back to the house, I wrote an email, asking for a deal to be done by the end of the week.

"Um, can you make it a little less harsh?" My friend asked softly, afraid of waking the dragon again. "Can I give you some suggestions?" We rewrote it together and I hit send. I got on my knees and prayed that she would accept my offer.

Dear God. Let this be the end. Let her say yes. It would be a miracle. I trust that she will do what's in both our highest good. I forgive. I forgive. I forgive.

Less than an hour later, she said yes. And I knew it was because I fully forgave myself and in the process, forgave her. She did nothing wrong and neither did I. We did the best we could with what we knew. It was divine. It was perfect. It was exactly what was supposed to happen.

If I act as the victim, like she did something to me, I will be the slave. But the truth is, I was not a victim. I created this lesson for my evolution and growth. I was supposed to go through this, no matter how ugly, painful and uncomfortable. I did this unto myself. No one made me say yes. I learned some valuable lessons:

- I owned my self-worth.
- I learned to create an advisory board for any important decisions in my life and business.

- I let go of shame around money by telling my parents about my debt and my agreement with her. My dad said to me: *"Can you trust that I have thirty-five years of experience running a successful business and can help you with these types of business decisions? Can you ask me for help next time?"*
- I saw my old pattern of self-sabotage.
- I saw where I was responsible.
- I got to experience forgiveness.
- had a new awareness around partnership in life and business.

The truth was, jealousy ate me alive and I suffered as a result. I was jealous during that time that she owned her worth and I didn't. I fell into victim mode, which debilitated me and sent me in a downward spiral.

As I write this, the old guilt and shame comes up. I am afraid to publish this. I am afraid of making her seem like she did something to me. The truth is, she did nothing wrong. The truth is I am eternally grateful for this experience. Because of it, I am a better woman. Because of it, I have opened my heart wider. Because of her, I got one of my karmic lessons complete.

She is me. I am her. She is magnificent. A blessing. A gift. A beautiful Queen, High Priestess and Goddess. That woman is the embodiment of self-love and self-care. I have learned a great lesson in what it means to be a woman from her. Thank you. This is my honoring and tribute to her greatness. It took me a while to get to this point, and it would not serve to lie about the journey.

The shame only lives in the dark closet of the mind. The shame continues to exist until we shed light on it. I have to write this. I have to release any last remnants of shame. *This is the process of purification. To let go of all that is not yours. To let go of all that does not serve the highest good.*

We have clung onto all sorts of "defilements" as Goenka calls them when teaching Vipassana. The different aspects of fear: worry, guilt, shame, hate, irritation, frustration. It is not real and it is not yours, but you are holding onto it.

This is not who I am, this is what I learned.

The jealousy, insecurity … all those thoughts rooted in fear and scarcity must be purified, ripped out from the root, scrubbed clean so that you can see the essence of who you are, the bright shiny diamond underneath the rough. Truth. Love. Purity.

Burn, baby, burn. Let it all go.

Purification begins with an awareness and identification, feeling the feelings that arise that you have stuffed down and suppressed as you took on the story that you are not good enough and imprinted into your cellular memory as "Truth." But it is not the truth. Identify it. Feel it. And then let it go.

You did nothing wrong. There is nothing wrong with you.

I forgive myself.
I forgive myself for saying yes to agreements to please and pacify others.
I forgive myself for having a big ego and overwhelming myself.
I forgive myself for staying in relationships too long.
I forgive myself for saying angry words to others.

I forgive myself.
I forgive myself for hiding and avoiding.
I forgive myself for quitting.
I forgive myself for fighting.
I forgive myself for being in debt.

I forgive myself.
I forgive myself for anything that may have caused others any harm.
I forgive myself for being so hard on myself.
I forgive myself for not loving myself.
I forgive myself for sabotaging my body, my dreams, my relationships, my work.

I forgive myself.
I forgive myself.
I forgive myself.
I forgive myself.
I forgive myself for I have not sinned.

I love you, Tanya Lynn. You are amazing for being such a good friend, sister, daughter, lover, mentor, teacher, woman. Thank you for being.

I forgive you.
I forgive you for all the times you blamed me.
I forgive you for making me the scapegoat.
I forgive you for throwing me under the bus.
I forgive you for projecting onto me.

I forgive you.
I forgive you for forgetting me.
I forgive you for leaving me out.
I forgive you for not inviting me.
I forgive you for abandoning me.
I forgive you.
I forgive you for giving up on me.
I forgive you for hurting me.
I forgive you for being angry with me.
I forgive you for being selfish.

I forgive you.
I forgive you.
I forgive you.
I forgive you.
I forgive you for you have not sinned.

I love you, tribe. I get that you have my back. Thank you for supporting me, loving me, holding me, forgiving me, caring for me. You are my family. You are my tribe.

I forgive them.
I forgive them for being unconscious.
I forgive them for trashing the oceans, the land, the forests, and the air.
I forgive them for forcing people from their homes.
I forgive them for raping women and children and pillaging villages.

I forgive them.
I forgive them for causing war.
I forgive them for killing the innocent.
I forgive them for torturing the captured.
I forgive them for genocide, homicide, suicide.

I forgive them.
I forgive them for poisoning our food.
I forgive them for creating the rat race.
I forgive them for creating this system of slavery.
I forgive them for fighting and fighting and fighting.
I forgive them.
I forgive them.
I forgive them.
I forgive them.
I forgive them, for they have not sinned.

I forgive you, humanity. You have forgotten who you are. You have done nothing wrong. You have acted out of fear and scarcity. You struggle for power and have not found peace within. I love you as my brother, my sister, my family no matter what you have done.

There is nothing wrong.
There is nothing wrong.

There is nothing wrong.
There is nothing wrong.

I am you. You are me.
I am the world. You are the world.
I am humanity. You are humanity.
I am them. They are me.

The disease is *dis-ease* – uneasiness with the internal struggle for peace and love against fear and scarcity; uncomfortable with the truth; reflecting and projecting the past onto the present.

Get that *all is well*. There is nothing to fix. There is everything to forgive. And it starts from within. When you can begin to understand the perfection in what you think is "wrong" or "bad" or "evil," you can find forgiveness in your heart.

When you can begin to understand the cause and effect of all thoughts, words and actions, you can find forgiveness in your heart. When you can start to see that the world is a mirror of you, you can find forgiveness in your heart.

When you can finally get that you have done nothing wrong, you can find forgiveness in your heart. When you can see that every mistake you have made was actually a lesson and an opportunity to find truth, you can find forgiveness in your heart.

Let go of bad and wrong.
Let go of beating yourself up.
Let go of the struggle.
Let go of punishment.
Let go of holding yourself hostage.
Let go of bounding yourself in chains.
Let go let go let go.

Your freedom depends on it. Your joy depends on it. The fear is an illusion. Forgive yourself. It's safe now.

Sister Spotlight: Kulsoom's Story

I asked Tanya to give me some extra time to complete my contribution because I didn't want to force it – I wanted it to come through me. Indeed, it has been flowing through me all day. I have spent a greater part of the day journaling, meditating, and praying. After taking a cleansing bath I feel prepared to commit to paper what wants to come through me today.

Last night I tossed and turned in uncomfortable sleep. Nightmare followed by nightmare. I dreamt of an apparition; a blind woman. She said she was losing her sight because they did not see. Followed by a younger version of the same woman. She said she was losing her hearing because they were deaf. Who are they? Who is she? Why did I wake up shaking from this dream? Am I her? Am I not listening? Am I not seeing? I think so.

Yesterday my partner brought up the subject of scheduling a couple's therapy session. My throat tightened and I shut down. "I don't trust her," I said. He wanted to know why because we had worked with her before. I did several one-on-one sessions with her. Why did I not want to work with her? I thought of the jealousy I felt. The envy. *She's a privileged white woman, she doesn't get my story.* No reason I told him, we'll talk about it later.

As I put pen to paper earlier today trying to make sense of my thoughts I began to see how invested I was in being a Pakistani Muslim woman in relationship with a Jewish white guy. The words that danced before my eyes – my thoughts, feelings, and fears -- revealed to me that although I desperately want to just be seen as a human being, I myself see myself by the colour of my skin and the religion I was raised in.

As my heart cracked open, the words spoke to me and showed me all the places I felt stuck and afraid. In my pain I read the anger I feel towards myself for not knowing how to navigate this unknown territory of growing as a human being with another human being who is so beautifully different than I am.

I began to see how I want to be met in understanding and acceptance yet I don't meet myself in understanding and acceptance, nor do I do the same for my partner. How can I be the space for myself to unravel and become beautifully woven into the intricate tapestry of my life if I am not willing to be present with who I am in this moment, in all my darkness and beauty?

Since childhood I have been acutely aware of the barriers that separate us. I have dwelled on how to end poverty, hunger, racism, rape, war, and injustice. Only today have I realized that I have been scratching the surface of what it means to be an authentic, accepting, and loving human being who meets herself and those around her with understanding.

My amazing partner has already helped me grow in so many ways and now I see that regardless of where our relationship goes, this is a beautiful gift and opportunity for me to see the spaces in my life where I can lean in and open. The spaces in my life where I can forgive.

Forgive my cultural conditioning.

Forgive my religious upbringing.

Forgive myself for being afraid.

Forgive myself for being imperfect.

Forgive myself for not knowing.

Forgive myself for not walking my talk.

I am deeply grateful for the amazing woman who has sat across from me and my partner guiding us, being an ally in our love and growth. I see now that the practice for me is to look at my partner and see the man I love − another human being − not just a Jewish white guy. The practice is to see her as an amazing woman in her joy, beauty, and grace with which she supports us, instead of seeing her simply as a white woman. These are my hang ups and these I release. I sing them into a prayer and dance them away as I celebrate my freedom to be fully me.

It's no coincidence that this is what desires to come through me today. During my very first conversation with Tanya, I told her that I was intimidated by white women and expressed that I would find it challenging and frightening to sit in a circle of white women. Much has changed since then. I completed the Sistership Circle facilitator training program with an amazing group of women, and most of them are white. These beautiful women held me, loved me, inspired me, and grew me into the woman I am becoming. In the circle, I was met with understanding, love, acceptance, and compassion.

I get goose bumps as I write this because I can see their smiling faces around me. I feel the loving strength of their arms. The soothing resonance of their voices as they sang to me when I fell apart. I feel them because they are with me. They are me and I am them.

If you ask what I got out of Sistership Circle, this is only a very small piece. The fact that I sit here typing this knowing that it will be published in a book read by many other women and men indicates how much courage and self confidence I have gained. When I feel fear or doubt, I take a deep breath, lovingly feel into that part of myself and forgive myself for being afraid. The sisters in my circle continuously said to me "I hear you, I see you." Aho sisters! I hear you and I see you too.

~ Kulsoom Shah

Inquiry Journaling/Affirming Rituals

1. Write in your journal about a time when you sabotaged yourself. Did you forgive yourself?

2. Do so now. Write out a beautiful forgiveness letter for anything that weighs on your heart right now.

Chapter 4: Core Four Foundation of Self-Care

"I take care of myself."

One of my basketball coaches in high school used to say to me and my teammates: "You are a product of your parents." He meant it as an insult when he was mad at us and we'd laugh saying, "no shit!" But he couldn't have been more right when I think about my relationship to self-care.

I watched my mom get overwhelmed and blow up with frustration. I picked up what she said and found myself saying the same thing as an adult: "You guys don't help." "You don't clean up." "I have to do everything." No wonder I was so overwhelmed and stressed out even as a kid.

She didn't take time for herself; her life was centered around caretaking for our family. I learned to put everyone else first. I didn't know how to take care of myself.

No coincidence, when I went into overwhelm after my breakup in 2011, I moved in with my parents with the specific intention of "being taken care." My mother loved it. She wanted to take care of me. So I let her. But the truth was, I needed to learn how to take care of myself.

Sustainability Through Self-care

To be sustainable, we must first take care of ourselves. To clarify, we must be of strong body, mind, heart and spirit, also known as the Core Four Foundation of Self-Care.

Everything that I have learned from the sisterhood comes down to asking the following question: how do I get my needs met?

I have broken it down into a simple formula: Step 1: Identify what my needs and desires are (See PlayBook). Step 2: Express those needs and desires specifically and articulately. Step 3: Receive what I have asked for with grace and ease.

This chapter dives into an overview of our personal sustainability, and then the next two chapters specifically address my own journey in understanding and expressing the big two: money and sex. I think money and sex should be the focal points of conversation in the sisterhood so we can empower each other to overcome the shame and suffering that has unconsciously been imposed upon us. It's time to break the cycle and own our self-worth.

Self-care is your foundation to living a fulfilled life. To make self-care a priority, you will want to create daily rituals that you are committed to. It's important to master your ability to schedule effectively to take care of your commitments. *The tribe, as the well, is a place where we take care of ourselves, receive support and fill up our cup with love.*

Sustainability is the capacity to endure. In ecology the word describes how biological systems remain diverse and productive over time. Long-lived and healthy wetlands and forests are samples of sustainable biological systems. For humans, sustainability is the potential for long-term maintenance of well being, which has ecological, economic, political and cultural dimensions. Sustainability requires the reconciliation of environmental, social equity and economic demands – also referred to as the "three pillars" of sustainability or (the 3 Es). [6]

Thought leaders weigh in quite loudly about sustainability and women's role in saving the planet. As an example, the Pachamama

Alliance is a powerful organization standing for changing the American Dream from having more (consumerism) to getting that we are and have enough. They educate people on the dangers we are facing as humanity and empower people in what they can do to help save the earth. [7]

Another example is Marianne Williamson, who sums it up with her famous article in the Huffington Post:

Human civilization as we know it is like the Titanic headed for the iceberg, whether the iceberg be nuclear, environmental or terrorism-related. The probability vectors for the next twenty years are grim, and our job is to turn the probability vectors into possibility vectors... in other words, we have to turn this ship around.

In every advanced mammalian species that survives and thrives, a common anthropological characteristic is the fierce behavior of the adult female of the species when she senses a threat to her cubs. The lioness, the tigress and the mama bear are all examples. The fact that the adult human female is so relatively complacent before the collective threats to the young of our species bespeaks a lack of proactive intention for the human race to survive.

Yet how things have been has no inherent bearing on how things have to be, and I think we're living at a time when Western womanhood is just a moment away from emerging into the light of our collective possibility. Especially given the relative lack of power – even basic rights – given to millions of women in other parts of the world, we have a particular responsibility to speak up not only for ourselves but for them as well. And we are ready. Maybe not all of us; but enough of us. Western women should be a moral force on this planet. We should not be infantilized; we should not be pretending we don't know what's going on; we should not be giving in to the various and ubiquitous temptations to anesthetize ourselves. Quite the opposite, we should be taking the wheel of human civilization and saying to anyone who will listen: We're turning the ship around, and we're turning it around NOW. [8]

The question then is: How will we turn this ship around? When we talk about "sustainability" we think of buying local foods, recycling, using less fossil fuel. We think about how we can create businesses that value PEOPLE, PROFITS and the PLANET equally.

How can each one of us individually make an impact? And how can we expand the magnitude of that impact when we come together as a tribe?

It starts from within. Self-sustainability. Fill your own cup through self-care and self-love and ultimately need less externally because your tanks are full. The craving and desire for "stuff" (like a fancy car, diamond ring, or bigger house) comes from feeling empty inside, which comes from not feeling like we are enough.

Self-care and self-love are not things we have to do. Of course, there are practices and rituals to create the structure for more self-care, but it is not about doing more. *Self-care requires doing less.*

Sustainability, the ability to endure, to carry on, to live till we are 105 years old, requires doing less work, eating less junk, stressing less, and instead laughing more, playing more, resting more, having more fun. I had been giving from a place of burn out for too long. I had been giving from a place of proving myself and ultimately to the point of depletion. My health deteriorated. My adrenals were shot and my thyroid was dysfunctioning.

The push to succeed, the masculine drive for expansion, the need to "make it" took a toll on my body. The male body uses testosterone to be able to work more and take physical action. The female body, having less testosterone, has to go to the "reserve" tanks when empty – the thyroid and adrenals – which is why so many women burn out their bodies working in a masculine way. One woman in eight will develop a *thyroid disorder* during her lifetime. [9]

Dr. Christiane Northrup also links thyroid conditions to the throat chakra: women not speaking up and voicing their needs. Is this healthy? Of course not. Then why do we do it? Because we haven't been taught another way until now.

Sustaining the planet didn't become an issue until the turn of the century. Making the changes in how much fossil fuel we use and how much plastic we throw away requires an internal shift first. The internal shift has to be sustaining ourselves and getting that we are enough and that less is more. We don't need more stuff to be happy. We don't need more stuff to feel satisfied.

This does not mean we focus only on ourselves. Self-care is not about being self-centered and selfish in a negative way. Self-care redefines being self-centered and selfish as a way of giving back to ourselves first to then be of greater service to others so we can give with freedom and joy.

The airline attendant says before takeoff: "Put on your own oxygen mask first *in an emergency.*" I say, put on your own oxygen mask to *avoid the emergency.*

There is nowhere to go and nothing to do. Breathe. Self-care is a way of being. It starts with self-love. Love yourself enough to prioritize your wellbeing first above all else. Without a healthy body, mind, heart and spirit, you continue to suffer and be miserable.

Imagine feeling strong in your body. Not getting out of breath walking down the street. Being able to hike. Being able to run on the beach. Being able to swim.

Imagine feeling strong in your mind. Negative thoughts don't take you out of your game. You are cool as can be with a breakdown. No stress. No worry. No overwhelm.

Imagine for a moment never getting sick. No sinus infection, no cold, no flu, no cough. Imagine no cancer, no heart disease, no diabetes.

I have struggled with being sick since I was a little girl. The first bad episode started in middle school. I had a 105 fever and deliriously ran up the street crying hysterically in my sleep. I came back home, scaring my parents as I rang the doorbell in tears. I continued to run around the house until my mom put me in her bed. The next day, I was still so sick I couldn't get off the couch. Everything was in slow motion.

I developed sinus infections every spring. In tenth grade, I got mononucleosis. I remember crying in bed saying to my mom, "I'm tired of being sick." My acne was so bad I started taking Accutane, a powerful pharmaceutical that kept me sick the entire year. My energy drained. I felt depressed.

I ended up in a Chinese hospital for food poisoning at twenty, an Italian hospital for an urinary infection at twenty-one, and a Peruvian hospital for four days at twenty-three after catching Giardia and Salmonella. You could say that I had a weak stomach and was prone to catch disease.

At thirty, I was diagnosed with thyroid dysfunction. For the first time in my life, I started to slow down. I had chronic worry-stress-overwhelm-fatigue-syndrome. I'm making that diagnosis up, but it is what most people have in our over-stimulated world today.

I started going to a holistic doctor who addressed what he says are the four most important factors to regaining and maintaining health: physical structure, nutrition, toxicity, and psycho-emotional stress.

My health improved. I rarely got sick. I started on the path of truth telling and listening to my body and giving it what it needs. I stopped avoiding my feelings and instead started to feel unconditionally. Doesn't matter if it was happiness, sadness, anger or frustration; I allowed myself to go there fully into the emotion.

Truth telling cleared up my throat chakra and my thyroid problem. For the first time in my life, I identified my needs and started speaking up to ask for them to be met by the people in my life. We'll go more into truth telling in Chapter 10, *Weaving the Three C's of Tribe.*

How many times do you feel guilty for taking a nap, sitting outside and reading a book, saying no to a social engagement, or going for long afternoon hikes?

The secret to sustainability is rest and rejuvenation.

The secret to rest and rejuvenation is slowing down.

The secret to slowing down is giving yourself permission.

It's that simple: give yourself permission to prioritize your wellbeing. You will be more productive, more energetic, and more alive than ever before.

If you stop working so hard, you can enjoy your work. If you stop going so fast, you can enjoy your life. ***If you stop trying to make it, you can finally realize you are already there.*** There is nothing to do, nowhere to go.

If you are constantly feeling exhausted, depleted and drained, you are not doing anyone any favors. This is how we exhaust and deplete the planet: we exhaust and deplete ourselves.

If we want to save the rainforest, slow down. If we want to stop polluting our oceans, first fill our own body up with love. It is no coincidence that our body is 80% water and mother earth is as well. We are mirrors. We are each a mini-universe inside the universe.

⁂

Wake up to your own energy source. Wake up to your own vitality. Wake up to your own body's needs. From this place of self-centered, grounded, conscious relationship to ourselves, we can then interact with the world and sustain the world, from embodiment instead of a bunch of talking heads.

I'm saying yes to ME today. Saying yes to self-care, wellbeing, and filling my cup so I can give from a place of freedom and joy. Saying yes to my heart's desire. I can't be of service to anyone (including myself) if I'm burned out, depleted, exhausted, contracted and an emotional mess. Time to recharge the batteries. Time to fall back in love with myself and radiate that love to others.

Self-love starts with connection to source. You are infinite love. You are infinite light. You are one with the universe. You are one with God, whatever God means to you.

There is no separation between you and the divine. Life is source. Look up at the sky, the vastness and expansion of the universe. Look out at the ocean, the vastness and expansion beyond your viewpoint.

We are but a grain of sand in the universe, a drop of water. And yet a whole grain, a whole drop. Magnificent in the existence of itself as separate and unique. Magnificent in its connection to the other grains of sand and drops of water to make up a much larger world.

When you get how powerful you are as a whole, intricately designed human being, you can start to see the magnitude of your presence. Can you see how mysterious and magical the human body is? We still cannot understand it. We still cannot fathom how the universe works. And yet look at the similarities. Look at the functionality and the brilliance in the design.

Can you see how magical you are? The times when it feels like magic because you manifested a dream or desire? How easily you can get what you want sometimes?

Can you feel those times when you've been so happy? Can you feel that first time you kissed someone and felt that tingle in your body? Can you tap back into the joy in this moment?

What a wonder it is that we can feel all of these emotions, the full range. How powerful we are in our capacity to feel. What a wonder it is that we experience so much in our lifetime. How fortunate we are to be able to walk and talk and think and play and feel.

In this moment of gratitude, we tap into source, in awe of the magnitude of the universe in which we live. Inexplicable, and yet that's what makes it so divine. This is what faith is. Faith is trusting without knowing. When we can have faith and trust, we let go of control and we experience the divine nature of our lives. You just can't explain how life works, it just does, as one intricately woven web of existence.

To love is to trust. To love is to have faith. To love is to let go. To love is to surrender to the divine. To love is to live in this present moment and have gratitude for being right here.

Love yourself because you were born.
Love yourself because you are.
Love yourself because you made it this far.
Love yourself just because.

Every day, practice loving yourself simply by loving yourself; doing nothing; sitting under a tree and looking up at the sky; feeling the earth under your feet.

Love yourself because you've done your best given what you know. Love yourself because you keep showing up every day on this planet. Love yourself for being born right now at this time in history. You were given special instructions to be you and love yourself for simply being.

If you need some practices for self-love, treat yourself like you would your favorite lover. Interact with yourself as if you were your best friend. Start to notice how harsh you are, how mean you are, how hard you are on yourself and call yourself out on it.

Every time you put yourself down, give yourself a compliment. Every time you beat yourself up, give yourself a pat on the back or a big hug. Every time you feel financial scarcity, give yourself a raise. Every time you feel like you are not enough, remind yourself that you are amazing.

It takes discipline. It takes courage. It takes awareness. It takes conscious action. And then day-by-day, it becomes easier to love yourself. You can start to cultivate self-love through self-care and then the self-care becomes easier the more you love yourself. They really are in a symbiotic, mutually beneficial relationship with one another.

Self-care can be cultivated through ritual and practices, but ultimately it comes down to saying no to "stuff" and to say yes to yourself and your wellbeing. Ask yourself every day as much as possible: *What actions can I take in my highest good? Is this decision for my highest good?*

My Rituals:

Take naps. Long ones. Like two hours at 3pm.
Who said the workday has to start at nine and end at five? Who said we had to work eight hours a day? Who said because you slept at night that you got enough sleep? If my body is tired, I sleep.

Get a monthly massage.
This was a tough one, so I forced myself into it by buying a package for the year. Massage keeps my blood flowing, my muscles loose, and my body relaxed.

Get a weekly chiropractic adjustment.
I thought the chiropractor was a hoax. I had a bad experience and felt ripped off and decided adjustments weren't for me. My holistic doctor did chiropractic but not the adjustment so I thought that since he didn't do it, it wasn't the best method. But my spine was out of alignment and my neck was so stiff. My friend gave me an irresistible deal and I said yes. My energy improved. The range of motion in my neck improved. My digestion even improved. I am hooked.

Take a daily walk in nature.
My best ideas have come on walks. My biggest inspiration comes from being on a dirt trail. I love finding new trails in my city and when I travel. I love hugging redwoods in Northern California. I love taking photos at places like "Potato Chip Rock." I love going barefoot on the sand walking the dog.

Free-flow journal three pages every morning to clear my mind.
This ritual came from *The Artist's Way* and has unlocked my creativity, extinguished my anxiety and been inspiration for countless aha's. [10]

Soak in the Jacuzzi, hot springs, or a bath tub.
I discovered Harbin Hot Springs, a clothing-optional retreat center, and have brought countless friends to discover the power of public nudity in becoming more fully self-expressed, self-confident and connected to humanity. Since I live twelve and a half hours from Harbin, I go in the Jacuzzi in my backyard as much as possible under the stars. I love reading a book in a sea salt bath.

Exercise first thing in the morning except when I'm on my period.
I love to alternate between yoga, Barre Method, and hiking every morning except when I'm on my period because I want to rest and take care of myself when I am shedding. If I don't exercise in the morning, it won't get done. This way, it's in the schedule and nothing comes before it.

Sit in a 10-day Vipassana course every August.
I started the ten-day annual practice in 2008 and have made a life-long commitment to never skip a year after I did a three-day instead of a ten-day in 2010.

Dance weekly.
I started going to Dance Church on Sunday afternoons where community comes to dance, play and hula hoop. I learned how to dance freely, not worry about what other people think and not need a partner to dance wild and crazy. It has been a great way to let go of the week and get my energy pumping for the next.

Circle with sisterhood weekly.
I am amazed at how much a sisterhood circle fills my cup and leaves me feeling energized, especially when I have felt like I had to drag my feet to get there. I remember one time when I had a migraine coming so I turned the car around to come home because it was getting too bad. I went back in bed and my boyfriend came in and asked me what I was

doing. I told him I had a migraine coming. He said that I needed to get to my meeting because that's what I needed right then. I listened to him and sure enough, when I walked in and started talking about my headache and then processed where it was coming from, it started to go away. By the end of the meeting, I felt so reinvigorated and my headache was gone. Sisterhood is a double dose of self-care medicine.

Practices I'm Cultivating:

Set boundaries.
I live in a community house (there are four of us and countless guests). I always had an open door policy for my room. I share my food and clothes with one of my roommates. But I started to learn that if I had no boundaries, I couldn't practice self-care. So I started to communicate when it was okay and not okay to enter my room. I made my room my goddess sanctuary and ever since I've held it as sacred, I hold myself more sacred.

Say no more often to projects not in alignment with my larger vision.
I want to support everyone and every project. I get easily inspired because I am surrounded by so many people who want to make a difference, but if I say yes to too many things, I lose focus and energy for my own vision. I need more space. So I can't say yes to every project that I get offered and every launch that someone wants me to promote. I have created a promotional calendar and a list of values that must be met for me to say yes. I feel into my body and intuition. I realized that the more I say no, the more I say yes to me.

Stop trying to please others.
If I'm unhappy, I'm not going to be someone who others want to be around. If I'm trying to please others, I'm compromising myself. When I communicate my truth authentically and speak in a way that honors the other person and they get upset at me, that's their problem. I cannot be responsible for other people's happiness. The more I can stay in my truth, the more I can give others permission to do the same.

Practice transparent communication.
When I'm afraid of disappointing or upsetting someone else, I tend to avoid communication. Then I find out that all they wanted was honest and open communication via phone or in person (not text, email or Facebook). A new practice I put in place is when people are reaching out to me and I don't have space to connect, I let them know I love them and I am busy or in a state of contraction and will get back to set up connection time when I cycle through to a place of expansion and space.

Rarely take a phone call or meeting before 9:30am.
Mornings are my sacred time. It's too jarring on the body to be alert and on my A game when I first wake up. It's easier on the body to do morning rituals like exercising, meditating, drinking a cup of tea and journaling. Give first to myself before I start giving to others.

Laugh more.
Laugh, smile, sing, whistle … use the facial muscles to lift the spirits.

Do nice things for others.
If I feel bad, it doesn't make me feel better to be mean to someone else. It exaggerates the problem. But when I do something nice and I put on a smile, my energy shifts subtly. It makes a difference to be nice.

Express gratitude and acknowledgements to others.
We all want to be appreciated. When I want to feel appreciated, I appreciate someone else and it comes right back to me. I love receiving a text from someone thinking of me or sending me love. I know they want to receive the same from me.

Allow myself to go internal during contraction.
When I'm feeling overwhelmed and need to slow down, I honor it. When I'm feeling like I'm hitting my upper limit of capacity, I acknowledge that to myself. We're all addicted to the high, the expansion, the joy, the bliss. But when we are feeling the low, the contraction, the sadness, the hurt, that's okay, too. It's a valid feeling. And it deserves recognition and love, too.

Manage my schedule effectively.
Without my schedule, my brain gets clogged up. If it is not in my calendar, it doesn't exist. The calendar is not just for appointments with clients. It is for appointments with myself. The better I have gotten at scheduling, the easier my life has been to manage.

If we are looking for long-term sustainable businesses, relationships and lives in general, our bodies need to be well-oiled machines, our minds sharp, our hearts expanded and our spirits strong. We need to take care of our greatest asset: ourselves. If you don't value YOU and treat yourself like a commodity, who else will? And if you don't value, love and appreciate yourself, it will be extremely difficult to find value and love in others. A tribe of mutual respect, support and appreciation starts from within. To take care of the planet, we must first take care of our tribe. To take care of our tribe, we must first take care of ourselves.

Sister Spotlight: Erinn's Story

When I first came to Sistership Circle, I was excited about what it looked like to connect with other Women. To share about myself, to open myself and to be fully supported. Honestly, I really had no idea what I was in for, but spending the next 9 months in Circle with these amazing women was one of the biggest catalysts to transform my relationship with myself.

This was the first time I was given permission to be emotional, to be messy. The first time I had permission to feel certain emotions, and that permission from the group created permission from myself. The shame of having feelings and emotions began to dissolve as I saw that I was not alone. This was a "shame-free zone" and the first time I felt like I was not alone. We all cried and felt deeply. We felt things that had been trapped inside ourselves for years, maybe decades, maybe lifetimes.

We finally let them out in this sacred space, and what we received in response was pure love.

Within this spaciousness I felt a completely new freedom, and I felt the power of my emotions. I felt their rightness for the first time and I began to release the wrongness I had been made to believe they were. I began to see my feelings and my emotion as Wisdom, guiding me to my own answers and transformation.

This was the beginning of the transformation and healing that has happened within my body and my heart, and this is what I'm here to share with you now: the power and blessing within your body. This is the key, the sacred resource you've been missing all along: Your Body.

What does it really mean to be a Woman and honor my feminine essence?

Circle is where I began to explore these questions and allow myself to play in this space. I'd spent most of my adult life operating from my thoughts and my brain - that's what I was taught! And in this sacred feminine haven called "Circle," I learned to honor myself, all parts (mind AND body).

A shift is happening, and our planet is moving more into a space of honoring the feminine. Honoring the feminine means honoring Mama Earth, our hearts, our sisters and the power of the grace and ease of Life. It's my belief that this shift will heal our hearts and it will heal our planet, by moving humanity into a more balanced state.

As women begin to trust their own inherent feminine nature, we slowly set the example in our world that these qualities are, too, worth honor and respect. We honor and respect them in ourselves first. We give ourselves permission to be wild, emotional, sensitive; to allow things to come to us with ease, instead of always pushing and burning ourselves out. We get more in tune with our hearts, our bodies and our emotions.

As a child, I was very sensitive and emotional. I felt A LOT. Sometimes I was feeling my own energy and emotions, sometimes I was energy or emotions outside of me (in other people or in my environment). I was shamed for crying, for feeling too much, and so I shut this part of myself off (or as much as I could). I stuffed my tears, my sadness, my pain and even my extreme joy deep inside, because it was not safe to let it out.

But, aren't we all entitled to feel our emotions? This is just one way our bodies and hearts process and release energy. Same as laughing; that is just another way of releasing energy. Once we embrace this energy within ourselves, we gives others permission to do the same. When we are out of balance (just like with ANYTHING in our lives) it can burn us out and disconnect us with our bodies and our hearts.

When we stuff our truth, our pain, our emotions down inside and lock them into a little box, they stay there -- inside of us -- waiting to be acknowledged. We carry them around with us everywhere, and that can feel heavy and exhausting, like a weight on our shoulders or a volcano waiting for the right moment to explode and release.

A new paradigm

I want to introduce you to a new possibility. To a way of living where you're deeply connected with your emotions, your intuition, and your Wild/chaotic nature. I want you to give yourself permission to feel. DEEPLY. The ups and the downs. The light AND the heavy. The happy and the sad. Because when we allow ourselves to feel the depths of our pain, we open up space for ourselves to reach new peaks of joy. We allow ourselves to process pain so we can release it. That way we're not carrying the weight of it around in our bodies and our hearts. We're not denying any of our experience or our truth. This is about honoring all of it and honoring ourselves. And from that place we create space and choice. We create freedom.

And so, How do we do this? How do we reconnect with our wild femininity? How do we reconnect with the miracle of the feminine spirit and body? By connecting back with our body.

When we're only operating from the mind, we're out of touch with the wisdom that our body has to offer us, and therefore cut off from our intuition, our emotions, and our truth. We're cut off from the subtle messages that our body is sending us in every moment.

When we start connecting with our bodies we notice different things. Our bodies slow us down every month in preparation for introspection during our bleeding time. Our bodies call out in pain after eating certain foods, telling us that those foods are not a contribution to the nourishment of our physical vessel. Our gut guides us to call someone or to make a certain decision. Our heart lights up, telling us we've connected with a powerful key to accessing our joy.

Our body is communicating with us always, and it is our job to tune in and listen and to receive the messages and honor them. We work together, rather than trying to control. Most women learn this at a young age when we start looking in the mirror and rating ourselves against the models in the magazines or against whatever standard of beauty we learn is "right". We start dieting in an attempt to control our bodies. We shush our bodies when hunger arises, we silence our bodies with medicine when we feel pain, we use substances to numb and escape painful emotions. These are all attempts to control our bodies rather than working WITH them.

Now, I see so clearly, we can work TOGETHER to create what we want in our lives. We use our bodies as a tool to feel how we want to feel in our lives. We can ASK our bodies for guidance. We can listen, we can honor and we can love ourselves in a deeper way than we've ever imagined. We can look in the mirror and honor what an incredible miracle the feminine body is. We create life within our wombs! When we honor the miracle that we are, we cultivate a deep respect for ourselves and our vessel. And that forever changes our lives and how we feel about ourselves.

This is the new paradigm.
Body, what would you like to eat today to feel more energized?
Body, how do you want to move today?
Body, what do you need in this moment?

Try this on for a moment - What if EVERY question you had about your life could be answered by you simply tuning into your body? What if all the help you wanted, all the questions you had, weren't answerable by doctors, and diets, and other people out there in the World trying to tell you what's best for you?

What if I told you that ALL those answers lie inside your body? Inside YOU.

What if I told you that the mysteries of feeling centered, feeling grounded, feeling clear, lie inside your feminine wild body, in your beautiful heart, your womb and your menstruation?

What does this mean?
This means, allowing your true nature as a woman to blossom. This means embracing your feelings, just as much as your thoughts. This means creating your life, your business, your money, your relationships from a place of ease. Disconnection with our true feminine nature is denying ourselves a beautiful gift. This gift opens countless doors in our lives. It opens the door to creating a life we love from a space of EASE. It opens us to honoring our bodies (whatever the size, shape and age we are). It opens us to eating and exercising in a more connected, and nourishing way. And it opens us to honoring the miracle and the grace of the female body and spirit.

For the first time in my Life, I look at my body, my emotions and my intuition as my GREATEST gifts and wisdom. Because now I know that feeling is our *birthright*... and our magic as women, bleeders, and wild creatrixes.

Now, pause. How does that feel for you?

I want you to tune in. What has this brought up for you? What is present for you right now? What is your body telling you? Pause, breathe, and take a couple minutes to journal or just sit in silent inquiry with yourself. Begin now.

What did this bring up for you? Maybe some new desires around how you want to live your life. Maybe it brought up some new possibilities that you didn't know even existed. Maybe it brought up some ways in which you've been living in your mind space and denying your feminine. Maybe you need to mourn that, I know I did. Maybe you're seeing some ways in which you've made yourself wrong in the past for being wild, messy, emotional, sensitive and chaotic. Until now.

Give yourself full permission to FEEL. Because this is the KEY to being more connected with yourself than ever before. Slow down, get quiet, and listen. Your body is beckoning you.

Embrace it, Goddess. Because THIS is your magic.

~ Erinn McMurtrie

Inquiry Journaling/Affirming Rituals

1. Journal about your self-care regimen. Do you have one or will you create a set of rituals that support your self-care?

2. Create a goddess sanctuary that serves your self-care needs. If you would like more information about creating a goddess sanctuary, go to http://SistershipCircle.com/Sanctuary.

Chapter 5: Express Your Orgasm

"I bring to the world my full expression."

All we want is love and belonging. All that's in the way is fear. Put down the mask and reveal what's underneath. The rawness. The vulnerability. Love and home is within.

 Oct 3: Vulnerability has an edge. And I'm committed to blowing right through it. Day after day I'm stretching myself to speak my truth like never before.

Here's my edge:

I really want to talk about sex. Shame around sexuality. Pleasure in sexuality. My own journey in coming to embrace my sexuality. The connection between sexuality and spirituality.

It's scary to talk about this type of intimacy. We've been conditioned to keep quiet. And yet I feel that our sexuality is access to our essence, the truth of who we are.

Last night I sobbed uncontrollably after a "pleasure session." It came from deep within. No thoughts or images came with it. Just feeling. It ripped through me. I simply let go and rode wave after wave. It felt like the biggest release of my life, perhaps from years of suppressing myself – perhaps lifetimes of repression.

There is no coincidence this came up and out yesterday. Whatever this is stored deep inside of me is directly connected to what's in my way from fully expressing my truth in the greatest way possible.

⁂

Three out of four women have experienced sexual trauma. I had no idea how prevalent this problem was until I started fundraising in 2010 for *Jeans 4 Justice*, an organization committed to ending sexual violence in the world. Their mission is to give people a safe platform to talk about sexuality and create programs to build healthy relationships in high schools and colleges.

One by one, the women in my community came forward to share their stories for the first time. Rape. Child molestation. Uncles. Fathers. Brothers. Friends. Neighbors.

By bringing the shame out of the closet and talking about it, women found the courage to face the pain and heal, to become whole again. Through this process of sharing, women found their voices, their full self-expression. *Jeans 4 Justice* became that platform for self-expression, showcasing talents to raise money. Dance. Song. Spoken Word. Yoga.

⁂

When I was five years old, I had a friend, Ryan, who lived on the same block as me. We were the same age and played together. One day, he grabbed me, pulled me toward him and said, "This is how they kiss in the movies." He forced my mouth open and jabbed his tongue in my mouth, moving it around quickly.

Shocked, stunned, I didn't move. Finally, I pushed him away, wiping my mouth. "Eww. Gross."

From that point forward, I "let" boys do things to me. They asked to kiss me, I let them. They wanted to put their hand up my shirt, I didn't say anything. Down my pants, okay.

Was this my body? Or someone else's? I lost my voice. I sat there quietly, not saying yes or no. Part of me wanted it, to feel something like pleasure. Part of me didn't want it, like I was doing something wrong, something bad.

My experience with sex started at sixteen. I had been drinking at my friend's house with my boyfriend. We decided to "do" it.

No feeling. No pleasure. No memory. A few months later, I found out that boyfriend had been using drugs, shooting up. Although he put on a condom, I told my mom and went to Planned Parenthood to take an HIV test. I was shamed by the nurse and, even worse, by my mom.

"What's wrong with you? Why do you keep choosing these type of guys?" my mom continued to say to me throughout my teens and twenties. I decided I didn't want to have sex anymore. But I did, with resistance. It wasn't until my last boyfriend in college that I actually felt and enjoyed the experience.

When I moved to New York, I desperately wanted something deeper. I wanted intimacy. I wanted connection. I wanted to feel. I wanted something other than what I was experiencing of myself and others so far. I felt lost. Numb. Disconnected. Lonely.

Something else is out there, I thought. This cannot be my life. This cannot be all there is. I'd come home to my white-walled apartment in an office building near Wall Street at two in the morning, buzzed, turn on my TV and eat a quesadilla in bed, watching *Sex in the City*. I'd wake up on a Sunday morning, depressed, alone, avoiding the typical Sunday brunch routine because it felt so superficial. I craved depth. I craved truth.

Instead, I drank too much to numb out, went home with too many men to feel loved, ran a marathon to feel accomplished, and worked at a corporate job to feel worthy, playing the game I didn't want to play.

And then I went to the Landmark Forum in 2005. Suddenly, it was as if a portal opened and I went down the rabbit hole to another dimension on a quest to discover "who am I?"

At fifteen, I had read *The Tibetan Book of Living and Dying* on the island of Kauai while on vacation with my family. As I trekked Kalalau Trail, I contemplated The Way described in the book. I didn't know that it would take me ten years to finally find what I was reading about in my own life.

Landmark opened my eyes to new opportunities and there was no going back.

I discovered The Institute for Integrative Nutrition in 2006 and quit my corporate job to become a health counselor, starting a non-profit to teach nutrition and cooking in inner city schools, getting gigs at corporations to talk about wellness, and giving one on one and group counseling sessions.

I drastically decreased my alcohol and sugar intake. I dated an acupuncturist who taught me that I didn't need prescription drugs to cure my annual sinus infection among other illnesses.

I moved back to San Diego to start Tribal Truth. It was through the sisterhood that I finally tasted what I had so desperately craved: feeling empowered in my own sexuality.

I didn't even realize that's what it was. I thought I could only find what I was looking for by having sex with a man. So I kept feeling unfulfilled, disappointed, confused, numb, unfulfilled, frustrated, lonely, and desperate. The craving wouldn't go away because I didn't go to the root of it. The root of what I was looking for was within myself. I had never masturbated until I was thirty years old. I didn't have a vaginal orgasm nor did I own a vibrator until thirty-two. I'm sharing this because it is normal in our society.

According to Planned Parenthood statistics, as many as one in three women have trouble reaching orgasm when having sex. As many as eighty percent of women have difficulty with orgasm from vaginal intercourse alone. Most women require at least twenty minutes of sexual activity to climax. [11]

Why are we so disconnected? Why do so many of us struggle to feel pleasure? Why are we dissatisfied and searching, craving for something else, knowing something else is possible but unsure where to find it?

Because most of us have not been taught the truth about orgasm and I'm here to share my experience to empower you. *You cause your own orgasm.* It comes from within. It's not out there.

I was looking for a man to "give it to me." I was looking for a man to save the day. I was looking for a man to satisfy me. I was looking for a man to create intimacy with me. I was looking for a man to fulfill and complete me. I was looking out there.

When a boyfriend asked me to masturbate while he was away for work, I resisted. "Why?" I asked him. "I don't need to." When I look back in hindsight, it was the most empowering thing a man had said to me to date.

As I explored self-pleasure and began to speak with women in the tribe who were sexuality experts, I learned that I generate my own sexual and creative energy through my life force, or *shakti*.

And as I continued to explore, my sexual energy increased. It awakened like a sleeping giant. I turned the light on and inside, I saw all the places where I was hiding out because I realized that my sexuality was directly linked to my creativity and my visibility in the world.

I had been living my life from the neck up, operating and making decisions from my head, completely disconnected from my body wisdom. I didn't listen to my gut. I didn't trust my intuition. I didn't recognize my body's signs when it cried out for help.

To discover my own sexuality was a three-year process of releasing guilt and shame from my past, exploring self-pleasure and sensuality, understanding and reading my body's signs, syncing my menstrual cycle with the natural rhythms of the universe, surrendering to flow, expressing my creativity, and finally finding my voice to communicate my needs, wants and desires with my partner and the world.

Notice that the partner comes last. The partner will not arrive until you are ready to fully meet him in your power. We'll be discussing more about your relationship with the masculine in Chapter 12, *How We Hold Our Men*.

Releasing Guilt and Shame From My Past

The Scarlet Letter; Burned at the stake; Stoned; Covered up; Catholicism. None of it is yours. It has been passed down from generations, stored as imprints in our bodies, propagated by society.

It has not been safe in a patriarchal society for women to discover their sexual energy. It has not been in the government's best interest to let women find their sexual freedom and expression. There is fear of what may be unleashed if every woman woke up to her sexual power.

When you get turned on, you are so powerful. When you get turned on, you are unstoppable. When you get turned on, anything is possible. *Your sexuality is a key to your freedom.*

This all-important freedom is freedom from the confines of your mind, *because you are in your body, listening to your inner wisdom.* Your sexuality is access to your essence, the essence of who you are as a woman with all your feminine gifts and strengths.

There is another way to living, one that is full of possibility … pleasurable, playful, joyful, light and expressive. This is what I'm talking about when I discuss living in flow with least effort. Women are afraid to go there because of the hurt from the past. And not just limited by your past, but also the past of your mother, the past of your grandmother, the past of your great-grandmother.

You have shut down your expression, dimmed your light, turned off and cut off your power so that you don't have to feel the rage and the grief.

Rage at what they did to you and your sisters.
Grief at the loss of innocence, power and freedom.

Feel it.

I know it is scary to feel those emotions, but it is the only way through the guilt and shame that is holding you back from liberation.

I am afraid to write this. I am afraid of pissing you off. I am afraid you won't like me for saying this. I am afraid of you shutting down even more and saying, no I'm not ready for this, I can't go there, I can't feel what I felt so many years ago. And I'm writing it anyway.

You are not a victim. You never were. You have a choice right now to feel all of it, to integrate those feelings that were shut down, to experience the shadow that you have not been willing to fully face before because it fucking hurts.

You have the capacity to go there. You have tolerated much worse before. The guilt is not yours. It is the church's fear to control you. The shame is not yours. It is the patriarch's fear to control you.

Women have been shut down for generations, our powers taken away from us. And now, with the rise of the divine feminine, our Mother has had enough of the havoc being wreaked on her domain.

All of those natural disasters I spoke of in the Introduction? They are happening for a reason. I'm not blaming "men." I'm not blaming anyone. There is no one to blame. There is nothing wrong. It is all happening perfectly the way it is supposed to.

It is unfolding in perfect sequence. There is a call from our Mother right now for us women to activate our bodies, turn on our power, remember the essence and truth of who we are, come together, be whole, be one, forgive one another for going against each other, forgive our men for they did not know, forgive ourselves for we did nothing wrong, and **take action**.

But the action to take is not one of violence, force and control. It is not fixing, changing, or converting. It is a different kind of action. *Listening. Allowing. Receiving.* Ghandi did not try to force. He allowed. Martin Luther King did not try to control. He listened and responded.

If we want world peace and harmony with the earth, we must stop fighting and start listening. We must stop *reacting* from old fears and wounds covered with guilt and shame and start *responding*. We must stop *shutting down* and start *turning on*. We must stop *controlling* and start *allowing*.

World peace and harmony starts with you, from within. Know within yourself that you are safe; trust yourself. Know within yourself that you can create anything in your womb-space; you are one who gives birth; you are the creator of life itself. Know within yourself that you can let go and surrender into orgasm, to life's joys and pleasures.

✿❦✿

The powerful feminine doesn't need to assert herself and make herself known. She is felt by her presence alone. Her sexual energy is so strong and potent that she radiates it out, drawing all of what she needs toward her and she receives. She is so good at receiving. She is a magnet; she attracts, she allows, and she receives.

Your body knows what I am talking about. It is already responding. Close your eyes and feel.

> Feel your vagina. Squeeze.
> Feel your womb. Soften.
> Feel your gut.
> Feel your heart.
> Feel your throat.

You have nothing to hide anymore. You can let go.

Write out your shame story. Use a fire to burn it. Go in your car, turn up the music and scream. Allow the rage and fury to release. Allow yourself to sob. Fully let go. Cry until your tears dry up.

Find a teacher on our list here if you need support moving through past traumas: http://SistershipCircle.com/resources.

Go to Celebration of Woman to get in touch with your rage and grief and embrace your womanhood.

Exploring Self-pleasure and Sensuality

Sexuality is not the same as sensuality. I believe that sensuality comes first. Your ability to feel sensations and awakening your body to fully feel pleasure.

I learned a technique from a teacher who rubs lotion on her naked body every morning in front of the mirror and says, "I love you arm, you are so beautiful. Beautiful arm. I love you leg, you are so beautiful. Beautiful leg." And so on.

How can someone fall in love with you if you can't fall in love with yourself? What physical attributes do you dislike about your body? How can you bring more love and affection to those parts?

Do these things for YOU:

- Use essential oils on your body and in the bathtub.
- Take a bath with candles and rose petals, salts and oils.
- Admire your legs when shaving.
- Hold your breasts while looking in the mirror.
- Admire the roundness of your belly likening it to a Roman Goddess sculpture in the museum.
- Use Mint or Tea Tree body wash in the shower (I like Tea Tree Tingle from Trader Joe's).
- Get a massage.
- Listen to classical music.
- Plant a rose bush in your garden and smell the roses.

- Plant a garden.
- Savor each bite of a chocolate soufflé.
- Decorate your bed with velvet blankets, satin sheets and a down duvet.
- Buy a sheepskin rug.
- Wear soft, pet-able sweaters.

Self-Pleasure Sessions

Before you start having pleasure sessions with a partner, get to know yourself. Set a date at least once a week with yourself. Pamper yourself. Create an atmosphere that makes you feel special. Buy yourself flowers and chocolates. Decorate your room. Put on nice music. Buy some coconut oil and a vibrator.

Going to the Sex Toy store can be a fun experience. Ask the attendant for help and to show you different vibrators and toys and give recommendations for self or with a partner.

Rub your entire body with coconut oil. Start thinking about sex and the things you want to receive. Rub your breasts and play with your nipples. Make your way down to your *yoni*, or genitalia.

Yoni is a Sanskrit word with different meanings. Its counterpart is the *lingam.* It may be the divine passage, womb or sacred temple (cf. lila). The word can cover a range of extended meanings, including: place of birth, source, origin, spring, <u>fountain</u>, place of rest, repository, receptacle, seat, abode, home, lair, nest, stable.

Contemplate on this word and its various meanings as you touch yourself. Explore with no objective. No place to go. No destination. Just allow yourself to let go and receive pleasure. Get to know the entire area. Use a mirror. Don't try to have an orgasm. The intention here is to extend your pleasure for as long as possible. If orgasm happens, surrender. Don't force it.

I recommend using your hands so that you can feel each touch distinctly and you can pinpoint where different sensations are coming from.

These self-pleasure dates with yourself can be during the morning, afternoon or night. They can be a break from work or they can be a vacation on the weekend.

Notice your resistance. Put the date in your calendar. Ask a sister to gently remind you and hold you accountable. Doing this for yourself … treating yourself like your own lover, can be one of the most ecstatic and joyful experiences of your life.

You'll notice yourself more alive, more turned on to your passions and creativity, more turned on sexually, more bold and confident, more fulfilled, peaceful and relaxed.

You'll notice that people will say that you are glowing. You'll notice yourself smiling more.

If you have a headache, pleasure yourself. It brings the energy down from your head to your *yoni*. If you feel stressed out and tense, pleasure yourself. It relaxes your body and your mind.

If you feel depressed or angry, pleasure yourself. It calms and centers you, putting you back in your power. Love pleasuring yourself. Love your body. Love you.

Understanding and Reading My Body's Signs

I didn't know that my body talked to me until I found Louise Hay's book *You Can Heal Your Life*. In the middle of this book is The List. It tells you every possible meaning for an ache in the body.

I started to pay attention to where I had aches and pains. Instead of using Advil, I listened. I felt. I read about it in the book. I said affirmations and took actions.

The sensations in the body are a physical manifestation of the mental contents. Your pain is directly linked to the thoughts you are having. Pain is a sign. It is not something to run away from, but to read and understand.

The more I became in tune with my body's sensations, the more I could ask questions and receive answers. What does my body want and need? Instead of thinking about it, I would listen to my body's wisdom.

If I am tired, I ask myself: Do I need rest or am I resisting something? If I am craving sugar, I ask myself: What feeling am I avoiding right now? The best way to start engaging with your body in this way is to sit in silence and stillness for fifteen minutes (see PlayBook). Have you noticed anything? In this week's ritual, you will begin to write down what your body is saying to you.

Syncing my Menstrual Cycle with the Natural Rhythms of the Universe

I do not believe in birth control. Yes, it works fine to keep you from getting pregnant, but it completely disconnects you from your body's wisdom.

I was told in high school that I should use birth control to control my cramps and my acne. As young as fourteen years old, I was being taught to numb out and control my emotions instead of feel them. I was being taught to use pharmaceuticals to mask the problem. After having a series of migraines in my twenties, Planned Parenthood recommended the Depo-Provera (Birth Control Shot).

Here are some of the side effects listed by the Livestrong website:

Bone Density Loss

A woman using Depo-Provera risks losing calcium stored in her bones. Without enough calcium in her bones, the woman risks developing osteoporosis later in her life. Osteoporosis symptoms include bone pain, stooped postures and fractures. The National Institutes of Health (NIH) warns that women should not use Depo-Provera for more than two years, as longer use increases the risk of bone-density loss. The doctor may also check the woman's bone density before giving her the injection.

Major Depression

Another possible danger with Depo-Provera is major depression, a mood disorder in which the person has sadness for at least two weeks, according to Planned Parenthood. Symptoms of major depression include agitation, concentration problems, fatigue, sleeping difficulties and feeling worthless. Major depression can cause physical and emotional problems for the patient, and untreated depression may lead to suicide.

Seizures

The NIH states that while uncommon, some users of Depo-Provera start having seizures. Abnormal electrical activity in the brain causes the seizures. The symptoms of a seizure range from a staring spell to a loss of consciousness, which leads to confusion. Some patients may fall during the seizure, which can result in physical injury.

Irregular Vaginal Bleeding

Irregular vaginal bleeding is the most common bad side effect associated with Depo-Provera use, reports the American Pregnancy Association (APA). This form of contraception prevents the release of eggs from your ovaries, which can cause you to experience intermittent vaginal bleeding between your menstrual periods. Certain women also experience lighter menstrual periods while using this type of birth control. Approximately half of all women who use Depo-Provera for more than one year stop having monthly menstrual periods, explains Family Doctor, a medical website supported by the American Academy of Family Physicians.

Weight Gain

Moderate to significant weight gain has been reported by women using Depo-Provera. Data provided by the U.S. Food and Drug Administration indicate that, on average, women gain approximately 8 lbs. after two years of Depo-Provera therapy. Body weight increases typically continue with prolonged use of this contraceptive.

Flu-like Symptoms

Flu-like symptoms can arise as bad side effects in women taking Depo-Provera. These flu-like side effects can include fatigue, weakness, body aches, dizziness, headache and nausea, explains the APA. The severity of these symptoms is highest within the first few days or weeks following Depo-Provera injection. Certain women can also experience breast tenderness, anxiety or nervousness as bad side effects of this form of birth control.

Injection Site Reaction
After receiving the Depo-Provera injection, you can develop a skin reaction at the site of administration. You can experience painful sensations or swelling at the injection site, which can cause your skin to appear red, irritated or inflamed, explains Drugs.com, a peer-reviewed informational drug product website for consumers. These injection site reaction symptoms typically subside shortly after Depo-Provera administration. [12]

Why am I taking the time to write all of this information about the Depo-Provera shot? Because no one told me and I suffered. I took three shots and did not get my period back until over six months after I stopped taking it and after doing extensive acupuncture to bring it back. I experienced depression, loss of sexual appetite, and vaginal dryness.

When I started to share my experience with friends, I heard other similar, if not more horrific, stories. Sisters, we must educate each other. The more aware we are, the better decisions we can make for our health and wellbeing. We don't have to be trapped by the patriarchal system.

Some women think that it is a good thing to not have the inconvenience of their period, but your period is your connection with the cycles and rhythms of the universe. Your period is supposed to be in sync with the full moon and allows you to be connected to nature's wisdom. *This is the source of your body wisdom.* The more in tune you are with nature, the more intuitive you become. [13]

My last and final attempt to use birth control was the IUD, which I inserted into my cervix in March 2013. I took it out in August 2013 after constant cramping throughout the entire month for five months straight.

My body was trying to reject it the entire time because it did not belong there. It literally "plugged up" my creative flow and essence from coming out of me. My bleeding was abnormally heavy where I would go through an entire box of forty tampons for one period. I finally said enough. If I get pregnant, then it is meant to be.

Now, I'm not suggesting that sexually active women, no matter what age, should reject all forms of birth control if they are not ready to bring a baby into the world. But if you are having sex with a man out of fear of saying no, because you need to feel validated and worthy, to get pleasure because you can't give it to yourself, and/or because you are trying to please him in any way, you are seeking truth in a place where you may not find fulfillment. The answers you are seeking lie within. This is an opportunity to get real with yourself and stop an unconscious pattern.

Surrendering to Flow

Orgasm for women comes when we surrender, when we let go of controlling our bodies and just flow, to get completely lost in the pleasure without fear of what would happen if you cried, peed or farted.

Orgasm comes when we relax and receive, when we loosen our bodies and release the tension we are holding. Orgasm brings a cathartic release. It is like an unstoppable river that may evoke tears that you had no idea were there.

Orgasm may awaken something in you that you never thought exists. It shakes you to your core and what gets rumbled may be deep pain and sorrow. *Orgasm takes anything that you've stored inside of you and lets it go.* The pain, the shame, the guilt, the fear, the anger, the grief. Every time a man enters you, he leaves a part of himself in you energetically and sometimes physically. Every time he leaves you, it may feel like abandonment, and your emotions get imprinted in your vaginal walls.

Orgasm is my release.
Orgasm is my center.
Orgasm is my essence.
Orgasm is my power unleashed into the world.

Expressing My Creativity

This book has wanted to come out of me since 2008, but I wasn't ready yet; I was too much in my head. When I booked my personal writing retreat and sat down to write in Sedona in October 2013, it flowed out of me. The book literally felt birthed out of my body from my spirit. I couldn't stop it.

No coincidence that a week earlier, I saw exactly where I was hiding out in the bedroom and that it was exactly where I was hiding out from expressing my essence in the world.

The last time I had sex before writing this book, I had the biggest orgasm of my entire life (as expressed in the opening lines of this chapter). It ripped right out of me and I sobbed uncontrollably for a good five to ten minutes. As soon as I would stop, it would start up again. I asked my partner to lay on top of me so I could feel grounded as I heaved, streams of tears pouring down my cheeks.

I had no memories, thoughts or recollections. I simply felt the release of emotional build-up from years and years of suppression. The more I integrated these emotions, the easier it became to express myself and write from my depths as a woman.

I never felt as powerful as I did during that Leading In Truth retreat the weekend before my personal writing retreat. This is the power of the orgasm. This is the power of surrender.

Finding My Voice to Communicate My Needs, Wants and Desires with My Partner and the World

I used to be quiet during sex. No sounds would come out of my mouth. Finally, I learned how to moan, then scream, then speak. This happened while I simultaneously learned how to communicate my needs and boundaries to my friends, roommates, family and clients.

No coincidence. How you act in the bedroom is how you act in your life. It is a direct reflection. I had fear that if I spoke, I wouldn't be able to feel. If I spoke, I may get turned off.

So the speaking and communicating had to come as a stream of consciousness. It was like becoming fluent in a new language; I couldn't think about it, instead I had to let the words come out naturally. I needed to understand my body through self-pleasure to start to communicate what I liked to my partner. I also needed to use noises to express my pleasure, and the more I increased my breathing, the better it would feel.

I have been afraid of the stage. I've been afraid of stepping into the teacher role and being visible in the world as just ME, not Tribal Truth or another identity or personality, just like I was afraid of being just ME in the bedroom.

My partner helped me. But his unconditional love was just a mirror reflection of the unconditional love I had cultivated for myself. There was nowhere to hide anymore. There was no part of myself that I was unwilling to see.

Because I was on the path of integration and self-acceptance and had learned to share my dark parts to form intimacy with my closest sisters, I had a new access to my sexuality with my partner. I had no fear or shame to be ME in the bedroom. And as soon as I discovered the freedom with that last piece of my sexuality, expressing it with a partner, I felt the freedom to go out there and share my message in a bigger way in the world.

I am no longer afraid.
I am no longer hiding.
I am no longer ashamed.

The blossoming of my sexuality and the expression of my essence is ever growing and expanding. It is a life-long journey and I am committed. The more that I open like a flower in my body's expression, the more I feel confident to take up space in this world. When I am confident, I radiate as the High Priestess, and I am open and receptive to serve. This is directly linked to my relationship with money, which we'll explore in the next chapter.

Sister Spotlight: Caroline's Story

I met Tanya in April 2014. I attended her workshop when she was launching this book. I was at a pivotal time in my life and was drawn to Tanya's message. She spoke about speaking your truth. She spoke about the tribe. She spoke about what it meant to be in your divine feminine. Everything she was saying was resonating with me. She was so wise and yet so young. I wanted what she had.

Tanya hosted Ben and Jen Rode, founders of Explosive Sexual Healing, as speakers for her event. My life was never the same. I had no idea the sexual shame I had carried around for over 30 years was having such a negative impact on my life. I signed up for a series of sexual healing sessions with Ben and Jen. Through this process of releasing my pain, sadness, grief, rage and shame, I was able to embrace my sexuality and become fully self-expressed. I was releasing all the guilt and shame from my past.

I was raised Catholic and got pregnant at 16 from my high school sweetheart. I was forced to have the baby and give him up for adoption. That wound was the foundation of my acting out through alcohol, men, love, sex, shopping etc. I had a hole nothing or no one could fill. It was shame and guilt that took me over. I learned that we carry our negative emotions and sexual experiences in our sacral chakra.

The sexual healing sessions were primarily somatic in nature and I was able to release that energy and claim my power again. Life changing to say the least. No more playing small. It was time for me to share my gifts with the world. Up to this point in my life, I was still working in the corporate world. I was way out of balance in my masculine energy. I was controlling in nature and not flowing or allowing things to be. I wanted desperately to utilize my healing gifts with the world. I was still being rescued by men and not claiming my worth.

After these life-changing sessions, I was able to become independent for the first time in my life. I learned what it meant to be congruent from the inside out. For me that meant what I was feeling on the inside (emotions) was being expressed on the outside. I was being myself whether people liked it or not. No more people pleasing behavior from me. I spoke my truth. I felt whole for the first time in my life.

I hosted one of the first Sistership Circles that Tanya led in May 2014. Her book and the support of the women who participated transformed my life. I found my tribe. I had the support I needed while becoming a New Generation Feminine Leader. The circle created a safe space for me to be vulnerable, authentic and real. I felt like these women had my back and I did not feel threatened by them in anyway. There was collaboration instead of competition. I felt seen and heard by my new tribe. Women between the ages of 22-54, all coming together to empower each other. It was liberating. It was exhilarating.

I was asked to co-facilitate the chapter on "Express Your Orgasm" during the first Sistership Circle I had joined. I was nervous but also very excited to share my experience, strength and hope with other women. We all have sexual shame. I wanted to inspire these women to let go. To stop hiding and release their rage, guilt, and shame. I wanted them to embrace their sensuality, which should come first, before they can fully embody their sexuality. I reminded them that their sexual energy is the greatest energy they could possibly create. They are creators of life. They can use their sexual energy to create anything they desire. I talked about self-care and how important masturbation is to fully know yourself. How could a man pleasure you if you don't know how to pleasure yourself? I shared some rituals they can practice to learn to love themselves completely. I invited them to make themselves a priority in their lives. What can they do to feel their needs are met? What type of daily routine do they need to incorporate to experience their divine feminine energy? This is the time we take back our power and step into the divine feminine leaders we were all meant to be. It is never too late to claim your sexual sovereignty.

It is through the support of this circle that I finally stood in my worth. I finally felt free to share all of the secrets that kept me small. I claimed my power. I could be of service in a way I never had experienced before. I am so grateful to Tanya and the women who have opened their hearts and trusted the process. I have continued to host and eventually lead these circles in my home. I have grown in such profound and deep ways. My spiritual life is much richer.

As I continue my journey in assisting other women to heal, I feel such deep gratitude for Circle. When I am hurting, this is where I go. When I am fearful, this is where I go. When I feel rage, this is where I go. When I am full of joy, this is where I go. I know I can reach out and ask for support anytime, and the women in Circle are always there for me. It is family without the baggage. It is a way of life for me. I will always be part of Sistership Circle.

~ Caroline Andrews

Inquiry Journaling/Affirming Rituals

1. Journal about your sexuality and self-expression. Can you see how the two are tied together for you?

Chapter 6: Own Your Worth

"I am worthy of receiving."

Have you ever asked yourself any of these questions: How much am I worth? How can I simply "be" and not "do" when my livelihood depends on my making money? How much can I charge for my services? How much of a raise can I ask for at work? How do I take care of myself and others? How do I get out of the rat race and thrive rather than survive?

This thing – money – we have become slaves to it. We measure how good we are by how much money we make. No wonder we never feel like we are enough. Even when we have "enough," there is still another level to get to.

6 figures.
7 figures.
8 figures.

It never stops.

Worth

prep.

1. good or important enough to justify (what is specified): advice worth taking; a place worth visiting.
2. having a value of, or equal in value to, as in money: This vase is worth 20 dollars.
3. having property to the value or amount of: They are worth millions.
4. excellence of character or quality as commanding esteem: people of worth.
5. usefulness or importance, as to the world, to a person, or for a purpose: Your worth to the team is unquestionable.
6. value, as in money.
7. a quantity of something of a specified value: 50 cents' worth of candy.
8. property or possessions: net worth.

We strive for excellence, we aim to increase our net worth, we want to feel important, and we have come to rely on money, and more specifically, currency, to measure our success.

What is success, really?
What is the purpose of life?
Why are we here?

Is it really to become millionaires? Is it really to have more stuff? Or is that all a decoy, a distraction, from the truth?

What is this madness, this game we are all trapped in, including our government who is in debt to the Federal Reserve, a private bank? If you don't believe me, look it up. This system we have gotten ourselves trapped into is all made up. It's make- believe. It was made up as a means of control.

Can you free yourself from the pursuit of money? Can you even free yourself from the pursuit of happiness (by means of making more money)? Can you free yourself from the vicious cycle of make more, buy more, want more, make more, buy more, want more … never feeling like it is ever enough?

Breathe. Breathe again. There is nowhere to get to. There is simply the present moment, right here, right now. There is only an exchange of energy. Giving and receiving. A circle. In and out. Flow.

Can you fully open yourself to receive money from known and unknown sources without your working or doing anything?

Yes, I have to talk about this. Sex and Money. Two of the three taboo subjects of this book that we carry so much shame around, thinking, "Is there something wrong with me?" There is nothing wrong with you.

Before we continue, I need to make a distinction: Money is not Currency, although people frequently confuse the two.

What is the difference?

Currency is a resource, tool or technology that is used as a medium of exchange in the marketplace. It was created to make transactions more efficient (so that people didn't have to carry their goats around to exchange for eggs).

Currency, for you in the modern day, is the cash you have on hand and "cash" represents Money, but cash isn't Money. Money is value. To make more money means to add more value. To add more value depends on utility (how useful and beneficial it is to them) and scarcity (supply and demand).

The first question that you need to ask yourself is: How much money do I need to make in order to have enough so I don't have to worry about it? Honestly. Truthfully. For most people, that would be around $75,000/year. This would put you out of scarcity mentality.

According to the Census Bureau, the median household income was $51,017 a year in 2012. [14]

The average American household with at least one credit card has nearly $15,950 in credit card debt (in 2012), according to CreditCards. com. [15]

While aggregated data is often challenging to find, the recent Global Entrepreneurship Monitor (GEM) found 126 million women starting or running businesses, and 98 million operating established (over three and a half years) businesses. That's 224 million women impacting the global economy — and this survey counts only 67 of the 188 countries recognized by the World Bank. [16]

Women, we see that we have a choice and so many of us are going for it.

We want to feel empowered.

We want to feel purposeful.

We want to feel valuable and worthy.

We want to make a difference.

We want to take action and create a business based on our passions.

We want to change the world.

We were each put on this planet at this time right now for a reason, and it wasn't to pursue money. Get off the hamster wheel. Yes, you may stumble and fall getting off, but your heart will stop pounding so hard trying "to make it."

We are each put on this planet at this time right now because we are light workers and we are waking up to the truth. We are becoming more conscious to the fact that we are being lied to, manipulated, controlled and dominated and we know there is another way. Our number one purpose is to be in the natural flow of the universe, to know the truth of who we are, to remember who we are as spiritual beings in human form and to find a meaningful, "right" livelihood as a vehicle to grow and expand.

Our businesses, our careers, our jobs to earn a living are simply that vehicle. To grow. To evolve. To gain awareness. To become more conscious. To shed the layers of our identity. To shine our light.

These vehicles that many of us are building are designed to help more people wake up to their truth so that more people live in joy with love in their hearts. Yes, it is possible. And it starts with you owning your worth, knowing you provide value.

The money will come when you get this. It's not something that you have to "do" and work harder for. It's energy. When you own your worth and value, knowing that who you are is radiant and that you have gifts and talents that are unlike any other person's on this planet – yes you have utility! Yes you are the only one so you have created scarcity! But not the type of scarcity that there is not enough out there; there is an abundance.

If you are a chiropractor, you have a unique way of doing chiropractic … the only one who does it your way, and by simply owning this fact, you will attract the exact right people who need your service.

There are thousands of other chiropractors out there, and there are billions of people on the planet. There is enough to go around for everyone.

There really is no competition. And what if there is a chiropractor down the street from you? Instead of competing, imagine if you collaborated and looked at how you could support each other's businesses. What if you looked at the type of people you served and the type of people she served, identified the differences, and referred to one another? You could make money on those referrals and keep the flow of abundance.

The flow continues when you believe. You believe in your self-worth and value, you believe that you are supported by God, and you believe that all is perfect and well.

The money always shows up when you are clear on what you need and you believe in miracles. Again, I ask you: can you fully open yourself to receive money from known and unknown sources without doing?

In September 2013, I had $100 in my bank account. A month earlier, I stopped using my credit card. I got off the hamster wheel. I panicked, thinking I was going to crash and burn. But then I got clear on how much I needed, I opened myself up to receive and I prayed.

You know what happened? Money came in. I had confirmations from the universe the next few days that I was safe, supported and taken care of by God. I had been wanting to feel the presence of God and I got it.

For the first time in my life, I checked my bank account every day. Money flowed in. I felt grounded. I trusted. I stopped worrying.

I now have the habit of checking my bank account. I am managing my money, clear on how much I need, and creating a new relationship with money that is empowering and loving.

I express gratitude for it.
I realize it is an extension of me, my worth.
I own it. I am worthy.

You can let money own and control you, or you can learn to have a partnership with it ... giving and receiving ... flowing ... an understanding.

It's just like any other relationship: it starts with you standing in your power and owning your self-worth. All relationships become much healthier in your life when you have confidence in who you are.

Knowing that *being* is enough. You are enough. And as a result, you have enough. You have everything you need. It is all provided for.

As an entrepreneur, I've had to learn business skills. I've learned sales, marketing, management, accounting, finance, strategy, etc. I highly recommend taking the necessary courses to learn the skills that any business owner needs to learn.

But no matter if I have all the education in the world, the single most important thing is owning my value and worth.

You can't charge more money until you feel in every cell in your body that you can. And even if it says higher numbers on your price sheet, the clients won't pay it until you believe and feel in every cell in your body that you are worthy of receiving it.

Open to receive.

⁂

I over-gave for years. I felt that in order to provide value, I needed to give more because underneath it all, I didn't feel worthy. I felt that I was a fraud, that I had an inherent flaw that I needed to cover up so no one could see it. I didn't believe that *me simply being me* was enough. I had to do. Over do. Give more and more away so no one could see that I was a fraud and a con that didn't know what I was doing.

What happened? I was highly sensitive to any complaints, negative feedback, or people who asked for a refund. *What do you mean it's not enough? I gave you everything I've got, plus more.*

It fed into my story of "not enough." A vicious cycle I had to stop. So I stopped. I jumped off the hamster wheel, crashed and burned, but you know what? I got up again. I didn't let it stop me. I allowed myself to just be.

I owned my worth when I stopped doing so much and got proof that I could still survive. Not only that, but I had more time because I wasn't spinning my wheels and exhausting myself so I could enjoy my life.

I began to play and have fun. I began to dance. I began to write and be creative.

Inspiration came through. It radiated out from my being. People said I was glowing. They wanted to be around me ... not because of what I was doing *for* them or what I was giving *to* them, but because of who I was being.

The only way for you to discover this about yourself is through the silence and stillness, when you give yourself the time and space to actually look in the mirror and admire, love, appreciate and accept yourself for being alive. You were born for a reason ...

There is nothing to figure out. That's more of the doing. Get out of your head and into your heart. **Your body wisdom will whisper it to you.** But you have to stop to hear the answer to your questions: *what am I here for? Who am I?*

I can't tell you. No one can. Allow yourself to open to the answers from your own heart.

You already know. It's your job to remember.

Isis was the Egyptian high priestess moon goddess, simultaneously motherly and businesslike, also known as a goddess of Divine magic and alchemy. Whether or not you believe in past lives doesn't matter. Your soul chose this life for a very specific reason. You have been gravitating toward your soul family to support you with your mission.

You have a vision of what you want the world to look like. If you close your eyes, you can imagine it. Now connect the dots of your life. What are the themes? What are the skills you learned along the way? What talents have you developed? What passions have you had since childhood, maybe even forgotten about? What lights you up?

It extends far past this lifetime. It goes back many generations. In stillness and silence, ask yourself, *why did I come here?* Whatever images, words and sounds appear, write them down. When the doubt arises, say, "releasing doubt." When the fear arises, say "releasing fear."

The more aware and awake you get as you sit in stillness, the clearer the answers will come. So often, we want someone to help and answer the questions for us. We seek validation and confirmation outside of us. *I'm here to tell you that you know. Trust that you know. Believe that you know.*

When you ask for outside assistance, someone may lead you in another direction, encouraging you, excited because they are a visionary themselves and feel like they know you. They may be spot on. To go on that route is okay; it is all part of your journey. All paths lead in the same direction. But I invite you to check in with yourself and your internal compass.

We are being called as a sisterhood to support each other in finding the answers from within. To hold space for one another to discover her essence and truth on her own. To listen. To love. To support each other in our own growth and expansion. We will explore the sisterhood in the next section.

Sister Spotlight: Jolie's Story

At 24 years old, I thought had it all. The diamond ring on my finger, living in a million dollar beach house, the successful fiance, and a bright future with my life coaching business.

My future was entirely planned out. I knew when I would have children, how many millions of dollars my fiancé's software company was going to sell for, which exotic vacations I was going to enjoy, and how I was going to save my family and take care of all of them financially.

The last thing I expected was to come home from a 3-days women's retreat to my fiancé requesting that we "transition out of a romantic partnership."

I was totally confused. Stunned. I couldn't even speak. I've never felt the feeling of falling so hard in my life. Like the rug was completely ripped out from under me.

This future that I created in my head was so REAL, so solid, so seemingly promised. How can something that seems so concrete just vanish in a moment?

I turned 25 years old a few days later and I had to ask myself some hard questions:

What is my worth in the world without the status of money?

What is my worth in the world as a single young woman?
And the loudest question in my head was:
**How the fuck am I going to support myself on my inconsistent $600/
month income from my coaching business?**
The word *scared* doesn't even come close to encompassing how I
felt.

My entire identity was in question and I had to get into some
serious action if I wanted to be able to take care of myself.

If you would have asked me about self-worth when I was in my
relationship, I would have boasted a confident YES. Yes I believe in my
own worth!

I would have gave you the laundry list of things I had in my life
that proved that I was living as a woman owning her worth. Worthy of
receiving a BMW to drive, first-class international trips, and the fancy
life. I hadn't a clue on what being worthy truly was.

As soon as I lost the identity of my relationship, where I had created
the illusion of lifelong safety and support, I realized that I had very
little self-worth. This was a huge wakeup call. I told myself that as a life
coach, I should have known better! I made myself incredibly wrong for
feeling unworthy and alone.

I knew I had extremely low self-worth because I felt like crap, didn't
trust myself, and lived in fear. Living in this state, it's incredibly hard to
feel safe, relaxed, and in the mindset of possibility.

My life was built on a foundation of quicksand. All of my worth
and identity was build on one thing: my relationship. I put all my eggs
in one basket.

I knew I needed help if I was going to get myself out of this negative
spiral I was in.

Everything changed in my world when I let my sisters support me
through this big transition. And not just the kind of friends that said
"Your Ex is such a dick! I can't believe he did that to you. You should
cut him out of your life."

Instead of that kind of "support" that is grounded in fear, I found sister support grounded in love.

I found this in Sistership Circle. It was like I was falling through the sky, full of fear and doubt, having recurring nightmares of becoming a bag lady, and then I landed in the arms of 15 loving women who just accepted me as I was.

When I joined Circle, I had no idea that I would be on a 3-month intensive journey to step back into my self-worth and truest self.

It was the greatest gift I could have ever imagined. Each week, I got to share with the group where I was in my healing journey. What my greatest wins were, and where I was still holding myself back. Over the course of the circle, I truly felt like I found myself, the woman who was always there. I came out of hiding.

There is something truly special about witnessing yourself speak in front of a group, especially in topics of high vulnerability and being completely held in love and compassion. I learned that I wasn't alone. Every single woman had her own story and low points she was working through.

Since then, I have an entirely new meaning of self-worth.

A woman owning her self-worth is a woman who knows she is worthy to take up space in the world. She believes herself to be a contribution and is confident that her words and actions help other people. She believes that she is worthy to receive all the abundance in this world. She allows herself to be loved, heard, and supported by others. She wakes up in the morning and has a deep inner knowing that she has a purpose for being alive.

With this new understanding of my own self-worth, I got into action to make my dreams a reality. I started trusting myself and taking risks.

I started saying said YES to a lot of things that scared me to my core and challenged my entire view of myself. I went to Burning Man, did a 30-hour one-on-one inner child healing intensive, did several guided medicine journeys, hired 3 coaches and energy healers, and became incredibly curious about finding myself.

I wrote a book called Empowered, Sexy and Free and became a #1 best-selling author. I started a business consulting company to leverage my skills in sales, marketing, and coaching to help Millennial women start purpose-based businesses from scratch. And most importantly, I fell in love with myself.

If I could go back and tell my 24 year-old self what I know now, I would tell her to take a hard look at what was making her feel worthy. I would encourage her to build a strong foundation of identity in truth and authentic self-expression, the kind that no external changes could ever take away from her. I would remind her that the only constant in this world is change, and that in order to best adapt to the inevitable, she needs to value herself as an independent woman. I would hold her tight and tell her that there is nothing she needs to do or say, that she is worthy just being herself.

~ Jolie Dawn

Inquiry Journaling/Affirming Rituals

1. Journal about your self-worth and value. Miracles await ... believe they will come.

2. Journal about what you want the world to look like. The world in all its abundance is available to you, however that looks for you.

Part 2: Tribe

I am a new generation feminine leader.
I've gone deep down into the underground to reclaim my soul
Being my vulnerable and authentic expression is my goal
I use my fiery passion to cleanse and purify my self-doubt
Burning through this ignorance is what I'm all about
Layers upon layers stripped and peeled off, my old self dies
I feel reborn, like a Phoenix out of the ashes I rise.

Now, my sister, it is your turn to let go of the past
To draw a line in the sand and say "I am the last!"
... to play small, to stay silent, to shrink back, to be suppressed

Women, we will no longer be oppressed.
For when we come together in Sisterhood there is nothing we lack
Sister you can surrender into the feminine; I've got your back!

You are enough, You are strong
You've done nothing wrong.
You are a new generation feminine leader and in this tribe you belong.

I give you full permission to be YOU just as you are
Unleash your power, goddess ... It's time we raise the bar.
To take a stand for this dream of freedom that we've had from the start.

Chapter 7: Guiding Principles of Tribe

"I co-create with the divine."

By recognizing the divinity within me, I see my infinite power. Limitless power. I can create anything. I create everything. I am powerful beyond measure. Anything is possible.

Knowing this about myself, I begin to love myself. Accept myself. Respect myself. I am in awe of myself. What a magnificent soul I am in this human form!

I was brought to this planet at this time for a reason. I was born with innate abilities and gifts. I have cultivated them through my experiences. I can connect the dots of my life to make up my unique story that no one else can tell quite like me. I am so brilliant.

I have these unique gifts and talents. I have my own passions, quirks, and inspiration. I am an individual snowflake, simply exquisite in my uniqueness and yet one small particle of the whole. I am part of something so much greater than myself.

Knowing my brilliance and exquisiteness, I focus on my strengths. I cultivate them. I bring them to the table wherever I go. This is my offering. I am enough. There is no need for me to try to be someone else or try to be any more or less. I am in effortless flow.

In my flow, I meet others to collaborate and co-create with in the world. I recognize their divinity, their enoughness, their uniqueness as a mirror of my own. I am you, you are me. There is no separation between us. We have our unique experiences, gifts, talents, circumstances, backgrounds and in that diversity we find that meeting point, that mirror, that reflection. The interconnectedness between us and all things.

From that place, I bring my strength and you bring your strength. We are each a spoke in the wheel of life. We each make the wheel turn and move forward. We ask others to join in their unique brilliance as other spokes in the wheel and together we create a community, each bringing his or her strength. Each of us realizing we are enough and we don't need to overcompensate for our weaknesses or our lack because it is all there in abundance in our strengths. We have plenty. We have enough. We are enough.

Mother Earth provides. The universe provides. We come from this place of abundance in Co-Creative Leadership.

Of course, we forget and need a reminder of our divinity, our strengths, our brilliance, our mirrors. And then we remember who we really are. This is Co-Creative Leadership. This is the new world, one global interconnected community working together in collaboration.

I have an **awareness** of who I am and what I bring with me everywhere I go. I have **love and compassion** for myself and celebrate the gifts I have been given. I get that **I am enough**.

This is my self-worth. This is my value. *Am I ready to **embrace** it?* It's time. The world awaits *me* stepping into my leadership.

And in "me" I also mean *you*. For I am you, you are me. We are mirrors of one another. Before we step into the workings of Co-

Creative Leadership in a tribe, bringing in all the layers of sisterhood – commitment, connection, and communication – it is important that we really bring home the importance of the first section of this book.

In all my years of working with community, I have distilled it down to one critical key step: self-responsibility. *This is your life. Can you claim it? This is your body? Can you claim it? This is your tribe. Can you claim it?*

Can you own **all of it** as your co-creation with the divine? Can you see how important you are? How much you matter to the state and condition of this planet? Can you let go of cynicism and doubt that you are too small and insignificant to matter?

It takes just one person taking responsibility to start a revolution. It takes just one person taking responsibility to become a ripple effect across the world. It takes only you claiming your power. Your power lies in your ability to take care of yourself – your body, your sexuality, your money, and your mentality.

Before we dive into the inner workings of a tribe, I'm asking you to take a stand with me. Are you willing to claim your leadership, because that's what we've been doing up until this point. Empowering you to claim all of your womanness and unleash it to the world.

Repeat after me:

I am …

Bold enough to use my **voice** for good.
Courageous enough to **admit** when I'm wrong.
Strong enough to be **vulnerable.**
Audacious enough to **love** someone who hates.
Daring enough to **accept** someone who's done me wrong.
Tough enough to wear my **heart** on my sleeve.
Resolute enough to **take care** of my body.
Risky enough to **forgive.**
Undaunted enough to take a **stand.**

And I am taking a stand that we join together as one tribe on the planet right now so that future generations can look back and thank us for the work we've done in collaboration.

Go to http://SistershipCircle.com/ourstand to sign the New Generation Feminine Leader stand and post the meme on your website or Facebook wall.

The New Generation of Feminine Leaders

I am a new generation feminine leader. And I'm so tired. I'm tired of the corporate greed. I'm tired of the fighting amongst brothers. I'm tired of the blaming. I'm tired of the destruction of our planet.

And I'm angry. I'm angry that little girls are being forced into prostitution by their parents. I'm angry that education budgets are being cut for the construction of new prisons. I'm angry that people are resigned about picking "the lesser of the two evils" in an election.

And I'm so sad. I'm sad that the Hurricane is already yesterday's news, forgotten. I'm sad that so many animal species are going extinct. I'm sad that so many families fight during Thanksgiving.

I'm a woman and so I feel. I feel all of these feelings. It's what makes me who I am.

There is nothing to be ashamed of. Nothing to hide. No reason to shrink back and keep my mouth shut.

I am a creator, one who gives birth, and I'm responsible for the birth of a new earth, a new humanity, a new paradigm.

I have a choice. I can either choose to be resigned and cynical because I am tired, angry and sad, or I can choose to be fueled and empowered by these feelings. I can choose to take action. I can choose to speak up. I take responsibility. This is what makes me a leader.

That *corporate greed* is my ego feeling entitled to my own money because "I worked for it and earned it!" *The fighting* is with my own brother. Those *education cuts* are my own reallocation of funds. Those *animals going extinct* are my own desire to eat meat.

I accept all of these things. I own it all. I feel it all. I can love in the face of fear. I can smile after I cry. I can accept others for who they are and who they are not. Hate breeds more hate. Love breeds more love.

This is what our generation can do. Choose love over fear. Choose to co-create, connect and collaborate. Choose to lead in truth.

The first step to lead in truth is to adapt the 4 R's as guiding principles in living your life. It starts from within. It starts with you. It always starts with you. As soon as you catch yourself blaming someone else, look at the three fingers pointing back at yourself.

As soon as you catch yourself wanting someone else to "do the work" and initiate and go first, look within at your own resistance. As soon as you catch yourself saying, "I'm not supported," and "I'm all alone," look at where you are not accepting and receiving contribution.

The 4 R's are a great starting point to own your power. Imagine if everyone was committed to her own path and took 100% responsibility for her actions. *Imagine if we built teams and collaborated from a place of feeling whole.* This is a lifelong practice. And it begins now.

Self-Reliance
The reliance on one's own capabilities, judgments, or resources; independence.

It's up to you. You create your own limitations with the beliefs you have bought into. Think for yourself. Make your own decisions about what is true and what is false. Become independent by freeing yourself from believing in the status quo.

Self-Responsibility
The willingness to be accountable for all of your thoughts, feelings, actions and results.

Your access to the world is through language. Your word creates your world. You have created all of it, which means if you want your dreams to come true, simply have the point of view that they will, declare it is so, and take action in alignment with your commitment. You are 100% responsible for every circumstance in your life. You are not the victim of your circumstances. Life is not happening to you. Life is happening for you. Choose to see life from this perspective. Know your power lies in being responsible: the ability to respond instead of react. Practice presence to increase your awareness and ability to respond.

Self-Respect

A deep admiration for yourself and all of your unique qualities, results and accomplishments.

Love yourself for who you are as a creative spirit of infinite possibility. Respect yourself for traveling on this journey called life and enjoy it. If you are seeking appreciation, acknowledgment, recognition, praise and validation, find it within. Your ego wants to feel seen, heard and valued, which means that you may be giving and serving with an alternative motive to feel worthy.

Self-Reflection

The ability to recognize the mirror image of life.

Your world is a mirror of you. There is no one else out there. Create the world as a reflection of your self-reliance, responsibility and respect. When members of your tribe trigger you, understand that they are messengers delivering you a message. Don't shoot the messenger! Instead, dismiss the messenger and see that this thing that is triggering you is an aspect of yourself that you have not fully loved and accepted. Reflect on this aspect of yourself – the gifts, the beauty, and the strength of it.

Sister Spotlight: Chanie's Story

Co-creation is a deep concept. It can take a lifetime to fathom the potentials of your personal power, and the outer dynamics that work along with you in your life. I feel blessed being raised with glimmers of that concept in my early life that set the foundation for me to later expand my experience of divine co-creation within Sistership Circle.

I am, and was raised Jewish orthodox in Brooklyn, NY. I have memories of our tiny dim apartment with a dozen siblings, and all the challenges I had in that setting. There was a spark, though, a spiritual knowing that emanated from my parents. I definitely saw my mother's simplistic way of connecting to a Higher Power. She *lived* with G-d and the Torah (Jewish Bible). Although she had many hardships; including rearing a large family while dealing with financial challenges, I always saw her keeping her soft feminine demeanor.

Even though I was too young to fathom a higher power, and had extreme challenges with feeling alone and unnoticed among my siblings (who were many), it still instilled in my early wiring the search for the Higher Partner.

It taught me to think larger.

Back in 2010, before I met and connected with Tanya, I sought to facilitate a sister circle in my community. I put together a few rounds, and although the women literally begged me to continue, I was not able to sustain it and hold the container. I "paused" until the timing was right.

The summer of June 2015, I was introduced to Tanya, who I was told "teaches" circle facilitation. After the first conversation, I was immediately drawn to participate in the training, and now I can say, it changed my life. Tanya brilliantly created a solid structure that can serve as a container for any culture or background.

I believe that being in healthy sistership is more important than most women realize. I always knew subconsciously that I yearned for belonging and feminine connection. It was only after I committed to the circle that I was then able to understand and speak about the true power of it, both on a personal level and from a global perspective.

Now, when I work with women privately, I see that I was not alone in feeling isolated. I see how many women feel the exact same way. Aloneness seems to me like an emotional epidemic in our society. Living with co-creative awareness can be the antidote.

Co-creation is the awareness that in reality we *are* in partnership in this world. We *can* feel connection with others, and ultimately, with the Divine and with the Universe. It is the same faith my mother lived with that you and I can invite into our heart and soul, bringing us together in Divine love and connection. It is a dance of more than one.

It takes time for our minds to grasp the concept of unity. A young, undeveloped mind sees everything in the world very separate and distant. Spiritual maturity allows you to see the Divine thread that flows through all of life. The manifestation of the Divine "other," the co-creation, is within the realities in your life. It's the real outer aspects and the real inner Divinity.

Divinity is the soft sounds around you, the thunder and the cat right next to you. Look into the eyes of your child, of your sister in circle, or of your spouse. It's all part of Divinity. Your colleagues, your friends, your bank account. The Divine is manifested and co-creates life together with you. Everything is Divinity presented in different forms to co-create your reality.

The beauty is that the other co-creator alongside the Divine is **you** and your consciousness. *You,* too, are co-creating your reality. The magnificence of it is the gift of choice. Step into that choice, sister. Ignite your creativity. Lean into what's coming through you and to you and consciously create that.

Together with The Divine.

Together with your sisters; who are your co-creative Divine partners.

In Sistership Circle, part of the program was co-leading one of the circles. It gave me great practice to actively use the muscle of feminine co-creation. It turned out to be of great value on multiple levels. The experience helped me get to know my sisters in a new way. It was a fabulous personality test and personal growth experience.

I remember one moment in which I felt very triggered. When I think about it in hindsight, I can see my personal behavioral patterns. Every interpersonal interaction can be a mirror into our personality and conditioned responses. Co-leading helped me realize my old pattern of hiding; in a very subtle, non-conspicuous way I spent years stepping aside, giving the other the power. Of course, it is easy for me to trace it back to how I was wired; being one of 14 siblings, I learned that I was not as important and felt rather invisible. Sistership Circle helped me to heal that.

Through co-creative leadership in Circle, I also integrating my "minority" cultural differences. It was a challenge to me in the beginning as an Orthodox Jewish woman with a different dress code that is obvious to others.

During a live leadership retreat with Tanya, I schlepped pots and pans all the way from NY to CA to prepare my kosher meals in a shared the kitchen. I felt separate, different and wanted to be invisible at first.

But participating in rituals where each sister honored one another, and being received by the group just as I am, was extremely transformational and healing. It helped heal many old sistership wounds, too. It has opened up a new space in my heart to allow for the intimacy of relationships. It bridged the gap with my insignificant and significant differences.

I realized more and more the expansiveness of co-creating together in one harmonious world. I believe that co-creation synergistically in a wider range heightens its power. Sharing and learning from each other with love and honor is what defines true power. Learning a new model in Sistership Circle on how to co-lead in the highest, most mature way inspired me in this way.

Sistership, I believe, is receiving one another without needing to shape or manipulate. We each offer something we can contribute from our personal culture. Being receptive to what I can learn from you, without compromising the integrity of who I am, is feminine leadership to me.

Co-creation is a reality which You and the Divine as partners both shape and form into a cohesive whole. Conscious co-creation is the act of remembering this. Being in conscious sistership can turbo-charge the power of conscious co-creation and offer you the opportunity to create your life in Divine feminine leadership – the time is Now!

~ Chanie Twersky

Inquiry Journaling/Affirming Rituals

1. Prepare to speak boldly and lean in to your dream. What is it? How do you need to be supported and by whom? Who in your tribe is available now?

2. How will you exhibit growth in the next six months? What skills and talents do you have and what other gifts will you bring to full flower? What do you need in order to accomplish your highest and best?

3. What will you need to shift or create so that you are able to do what you love, be around people you love, and be in love with yourself?

4. Write in your journal about your willingness to be accountable for your thoughts, feelings, actions and results – all of them. *Breathe into this.*

Chapter 8: The Vision of Tribe Nation

"I am connected."

The morning of December 14, 2011, I was on the phone with a tribe sister, making amends from an argument we had. We are complete opposites and easily trigger one another. We were talking about the larger vision of tribe and how it relates to working through our differences by leaning in and communicating. Most people get upset and "break up" because they can't work it out.

Imagine if everyone could see the larger picture and work out their differences because they remember in the end how much they love each other and are committed to one another's growth and success.

Later that morning, when the Sandy Hook, Connecticut, shooting occurred, she emailed me:

Thank you again for pointing out the much larger picture of how, in doing this work with each other, we are able to have a much larger effect on the community and the world.

In reflecting on the horrific shooting in Connecticut today, I am getting your vision on a deeper level.

I'm getting that I can easily feel helpless in changing or influencing the aspects of our culture, which somehow lead to such unfathomable tragedies.

But I don't feel so helpless when I see that in starting simply doing this work myself, and with you and our [tribe], and then bringing it out to our families, friends, clients, communities, etc. ... That is how we change the world. I see it. I often have trouble truly grasping such a big vision – it doesn't come naturally to me. But this helps me see the connection in a way I can grasp. And it gives me a window into how I can have impact. And then I feel much more empowered, rather than slipping into disempowerment or complacency.

People wouldn't be taking such rash actions if they had the opportunity and support that we have to heal and work through our stuff. We get to do this work ourselves and bring it to more people in many different ways.

It feels so good to really grasp this. Thank you for holding that big vision and for doing this work with me. I love you.

What is This Vision I am Referring To?

Before I share this vision, I need to give you some context by sharing the history of Tribal Truth and Sistership Circle.

When I moved back in 2008 to San Diego from New York where I lived for five years, I hit the reset button. I wasn't sure what I wanted to do next with my life. What I did know was I needed community. I wanted to be around like-minded women. In January 2009, I put on my first event in San Diego and named it *Women 4 Wellness*. Women loved it and were amazed that I was able to pull together thirty women in a room, most of whom I didn't know. I immediately made new friends and found a sweet spot for myself: organizing community gatherings.

Every month, I brought in a new woman to speak about holistic health. By the time August rolled around, I felt disconnected from what I was doing. Something was missing. I wanted a business partner and I wanted to shift the focus away from wellness.

A couple months later, a friend introduced me to a woman who wrote a book to empower women in all areas of their life. We decided to collaborate and rebrand *Women 4 Wellness* to a women's empowerment community.

In January 2010, we launched with over sixty-five women packed into a downtown loft. You know something is right when things fall into place easily and quickly. Tribal Truth was the place to be.

A few months later, one of our members came to me with the idea of having weekly circles. I wanted to incorporate a 90-day plan to have the circles be laser focused on an intention so women could support one another's dreams. Tribal Truth took a quantum leap in June when we launched the first Sistership Circle.

We were onto something. The results were profound for the women in the circles. At the same time, we did not know how to handle the competitive nature of women, and so while deep friendships were formed and businesses blossomed, many upsets ruined relationships as well. We still had a lot to learn about circle facilitation and holding space.

In February 2011, we launched Los Angeles with twelve of the top experts in the industry and over 100 women in attendance at a gorgeous home owned by Hollywood's trailer voiceover guy. We were known for having events at unique venues like the Harley Davidson store, Rancho Santa Fe mansions, art galleries and chic downtown lofts.

At the same time, we decided to dissolve our partnership agreement. We had different visions of where we wanted to go with our lives and as my partner always put it, "You are Tribal Truth." I stepped into the CEO role and she moved on to work with another global company.

I took the model from the LA launch and duplicated it to launch tribes in New York City and San Francisco over the next few months. This time, I had a learning curve around leadership training. How do I teach someone to do what I do so well? I learned through many mistakes.

What I got was this: our business and the projects we align ourselves with are our biggest personal growth opportunities. To have someone be accountable as the leader of her own life, she has to have a strong "why" for herself, see the training opportunity as a privilege and live her life in alignment with her core values

As I felt a spiritual shift within myself and on the planet, Tribal Truth again evolved.

Something was missing. I was bored with the networking event model that we kept getting pigeonholed into. I didn't want speakers coming in doing their same old signature talks that they did on every other platform. I wanted depth. I wanted vulnerability. I wanted fulfillment on a soul level, not just a masculine focus on making money and promoting one another's businesses.

When I returned from India in February 2012, we launched Las Vegas and London. The team of tribe leaders and I began to peel back the layers and look deeper at what it looked like to be a real community, where women had each other's backs no matter what and were willing to look deep within themselves for personal responsibility and truth telling.

We questioned whether we were walking the walk. Collaboration. Leadership. What did these words really mean? How could we embody these concepts – live and breathe them – not just talk about them?

It was in May 2012 when I saw how much I was still running Tribal Truth on my own as a solopreneur and lone ranger. I was a control freak who wasn't empowering anyone on my team to truly shine in her brilliance. I saw where I was the bottleneck in preventing Tribal Truth from expanding without busting its seams and falling apart.

I had to surrender.

I had to fully let go of controlling how it looked. I had to stop doing so much and start trusting others. I had to start believing in myself first on a whole new level and start telling the truth about how inauthentic I was.

I had so much inner conflict and turmoil. I was an emotional mess. I felt like everything was being stripped away from me — my boyfriend broke up with me and I had to move out of our apartment, I totaled my car, dropped my phone in the river, lost friends and faced the fact that I had a mounting debt.

This was a turning point.

As I mentioned in the Resistance section of Chapter 2, they say that the universe first taps you on the shoulder when it's time to change something. If you don't listen, you get pushed. If you still ignore it, you get knocked out by a brick. If you still don't get the message, you get a terminal illness or end up in an accident where you are brought to the brink of death.

I believe this. I believe that the universe has been guiding me to keep course correcting. Tribal Truth has been a container for my own growth and expansion, for me to embody the work instead of just preaching about it. I keep going deeper and deeper and as I do, Tribal Truth's structure keeps shifting and changing.

In 2013, Tribal Truth evolved again with the creation of *Honoring the Masculine-Feminine*. The intention was to give men an experience of the women's circle. We formed a circle and held a safe space for a circle of men in the middle to share what it means to be a man today. The men bared it all. They talked about the lover, the warrior, the king. They got angry, they cried, they laughed. They told us how it was confusing to be a man. They were vulnerable. The women were touched, moved and inspired. *Honoring the Masculine-Feminine* spread to Los Angeles and San Francisco.

And then in June I stopped. Surrendering again. I gave up managing the women's tribes and had them go independent. I gave up *Honoring the Masculine-Feminine*.

After 6 months of a deep dive into my own dark night of the soul, Sistership Circle (the original offering in 2010) reemerged. The PlayBook outlines a 12-week journey through the chapters of this book, and provided a curriculum for "Circle work."

Just as I shed my skin like a snake to let go of my old identity, I knew Tribal Truth had to do the same by changing its name officially to Sistership Circle.

Everything at that point clicked into place and the vision started to manifest in its truest form.

This vision is for the women leaders of the world to come together to create a Tribe Nation.

While each woman holds her own circles for her tribe, she understands the truth that she is not alone and separate, there is no competition, and together in sisterhood we are stronger.

For the various tribes on planet earth to live in the new paradigm, we must shift from hierarchies to circles of co-creative leadership.

The women of the world will lead the Human Tribe as One Tribe Nation by first embodying this model of co-creative leadership with one another, celebrating each other's unique gifts as equally valued contributions to the whole.

By coming together in sisterhood, leaving no sister behind, we heal our old wounds of separation and create a container for the world of equality amongst all people and harmony with the earth.

This **vision** of Tribe Nation is rooted in the following principles:

Each person is self-reliant and takes full personal responsibility for her life. Develop a loving and compassionate respect for yourself and others. Reflect on your deepest desires and take actions to fulfill on your personal mission.

Create sacred space for true collaboration and co-creation. We are not alone. We are not separate. We are all connected and once we discover this, we can start to vulnerably share the truth. Through authentic truth telling, we can build trust first within ourselves and then with the people in our community.

Honor your own journey. We are each leaders in our own lives. We are each learning how to lead from our hearts and not solely from our brains. We are learning to connect instead of run away, go through the eye of the needle to get the exact lesson we need to take the next step forward on our journey.

Don't shoot the messenger, get the message. When you show up fully in the present moment and receive whatever comes up with open arms, you may attract people who mirror your shadow. Instead of blaming, judging or pushing this person away, thank him or her for giving you an opportunity to heal.

Sisterhood is a space for healing. We carry so many wounds that extend back generations. It is time to let it go and move forward together as one united community.

Reclaim your voice. To speak up after being shut down. To declare our truth that inspires others to do the same. To listen with openness. To allow one another to shine in brilliance. To claim our own brilliance when for so long we have dimmed our light.

Sacred Sistership creates real community. We work out our differences. We accept each other's weaknesses and complement each other's strengths. We let go of our expectations, judgments and prejudices. We stop trying to control, manipulate and fix one another. We celebrate the breakdowns and the breakthroughs. We embrace the darkness as much as the light. We have one another's backs. We lift one another up. We stand for one another. We lead by example. We call one another out with compassion. We are love. We are one. This is the future of our world. As difficult as it is to walk this path, we are committed. We know deep in our hearts that this is the way we create peace on the planet.

Tribe Nation

I have a vision of one million circles gathering on the planet.

I see women gathering in living rooms and community centers all over the world. I see women holding each other, hugging, crying, laughing, singing, dancing. I see women working out their differences. I see women empowering one another to go after their hearts' desires. I see women celebrating each other's new businesses, going to each other's weddings, rubbing each other's pregnant bellies, massaging each other's feet, throwing birthday parties for one another.

I hold the vision for these things because I have already experienced them in my own tribe here in San Diego, and heard about them in other cities.

This is a lifestyle we are already living. It is spreading. It will continue to spread.

Imagine all of these tribes of women gathering in cities all around the world, and they are all connected as one tribe nation. So they are not separate, but one and the same. Each one magnificent in its cultural diversity. Each one having its own rites and rituals. Each one filled with women of different race, color, age and education background.

Tribe is not for the privileged; it is for the everyday woman on her path to empowerment.

She is realizing her own potential to lead her own life in truth. She is doing that with the support of her sisters.

Circle is the meeting point of ancient traditions with modern culture. It is the intersection of spirituality, health, relationship and business. It is the place where we honor who we are, where we've come from and where we are going. It is a place where we wake up together to the truth of who we are.

How Do We Do It?

While being in tribe is the most natural thing – our ancestors lived in community for centuries – it has become the most foreign thing to the modern woman who has been raised to compete with her sisters, judge her own body image and hide her feelings.

So many people right now crave community and are going out there to find and/or create it. Tribe has become a buzz word in the new millennium for a reason: people are waking up and seeing that what is most important is connection. To be seen, heard, loved and valued. All we have is relationship and so it seems like the most logical thing is to work on removing all the obstacles from the deep connection we all crave.

My intention is to teach and provide the framework of Circle to help leaders create, build and sustain tribes, (whatever that looks like, i.e., groups, sister circles and communities). If you are interested in leading circles in your community, go to http://SistershipCircle.com/ebook.

I have identified three things to create, build and sustain tribe:

1) Create the need: identify the wound that keeps people separated and how to bring them together.

2) Build the foundation: weave the three threads together that create a real tribe – commitment, connection and communication.

3) Sustain the movement: practice Co-Creative Leadership, which maintains and sustains a real tribe.

Sister Spotlight: Sharlene's Story

In the beginning

Picture this: a living room with the sofa and chairs neatly arranged to form a circle, dimmed lights, a tiny altar in the middle, beautiful flowers and the sweet smell of incense. A sugar free polenta cake, drinks and me at the ready, feeling nervous and excited. With nine women signed up this was my biggest circle to date.

As I welcome the women into my home that evening I felt a sense of hope and gratitude. Hopeful that this was the start of creating the community and tribe I was longing for and grateful that I had somehow made it happen, and that the women had answered the call.

A desire for circle

A couple of months prior, in a session with my coach, I had a clear vision of what I needed in my life and what I wanted to create. I longed to feel a sense of belonging and connection, to have the sacred space to be completely myself, warts and all. Tired of the superficial bullshit present in most conversations and interactions, I craved depth, meaning, truth and authenticity. I wanted to be held and supported and to reciprocate this. It became so clear to me that I needed women, I needed community, I needed sisterhood. Above all, I needed a tribe.

Determined to bring this vision to life and to heal the sense of lack and disconnection inside of me, I decided I would start a women's circle – again!

Years earlier, in 2008 I attempted to start a circle for women in London but a month or two and about 3 women later it didn't really go anywhere.

Looking back now I realize how a deep sense of longing and disconnection is what motivated me to seek circle. However, my lack of understanding, knowledge and clarity about the divine feminine and about leading circles meant the vision did not take hold. I also had some personal healing to do. But as with anything that remains unfulfilled, unresolved and unhealed, my desires for connection and belonging did not go away. Instead, they surfaced and were re-awakened years later, only this time my craving was stronger, I was more committed and so much more empowered to make it happen.

So, in my second attempt to start circle, I put it out there and my circle started with four of us – one friend and two women who I met at the local Buddhist center. We sat in circle and opened our hearts. As we shared drinks, desserts and stories, we all felt a spark of aliveness about our experience together. Something felt so good about coming together in this way.

By the time the third circle came around, after putting it out there on social media, there were nine women who showed up. We gathered in the kitchen for drinks and cake before making our way into the living room, ready to begin.

A cringe-worthy lesson

What happened next was a total and utter disaster! It was the epitome of how not to lead a circle! I witnessed a lack of compassion and respect for others, a lack of trust and sacredness in the circle, cattiness, the absence of accountability and responsibility and a complete lack of togetherness. The wounds of sisterhood and tribe (or perhaps lack of authentic sisterhood and tribe) became so apparent. As the women hurriedly scurried out of the door and I breathed a massive sigh of relief and disappointment, that evening I made the decision that I would not lead another circle until I had the right skills and training. I knew in my heart what I wanted to create and I now had the experience of what I didn't want.

Hello Sistership Circle

It was through my intentional search for circle training that I was lucky enough to discover Sistership circle, and voila! This was the answer to my prayers and EXACTLY what I had been looking for.

I felt a sense of coming home as I was warmly welcomed into the Sistership Circle tribe. I had found a circle of women, women from all over the world with such diversity who shared similar values and visions. I had found the place where authenticity, vulnerability, truth and community were encouraged. At long last, I had found my tribe.

This was my doorway into authentic sisterhood where I got to experience what being in a tribe and circle was all about. I had envisioned it and longed for it and now this was my chance to truly experience it, and learn what I needed to take it out into my world. Being part of a tribe and circle has been so deeply nourishing and powerful.

Gifts of Sistership Circle

Throughout my journey with Sistership Circle I have learned how to embrace and embody my divine feminine leadership. After completing one of Sistership Circle's signature courses - How To Lead Circle - I was well equipped and supported to go out there and create the circles that my heart longed for. I learned the perfect balance of divine masculine and divine feminine and how to bring this into sacred facilitation and leading circle.

Sistership Circle has not only enhanced my continued personal development and transformation and understanding of the sacred feminine, it has also been such a great platform to launch me in the most solid and grounded, yet soft and receptive way into divine feminine leadership and sacred facilitation.

I am delighted to share that my circles and feminine leadership have strengthen and I am now, thanks to Sistership Circle, bringing to life a beautiful tribe and sisterhood in my own community.

Imagine

Amongst other wonderful things, Sistership Circle is so gracefully providing and holding the space for the vision of tribe to be re-awakened and birthed in our world that so desperately needs it.

Imagine what the world, or your community, would be like if each person was self-reliant and taking full responsibility for their lives; if there was the opportunity for each member to blossom forth to co-create and collaborate, sharing their gifts and talents. Imagine if we no longer felt separate or disconnected and instead we felt acknowledged, supported and loved. **What if we came together in sacred space to celebrate our light and to offer love, compassion and respect to our darkness and our wounds?** And, imagine if every woman in the world had a circle and a tribe she could lean into ...

I love being part of an organization and a tribe that is birthing a new reality founded on truth, love and harmony in our world – one circle at a time. And I love knowing that whilst I'm busy creating and contributing to my own tribe and circles, the reality is that we part of of a bigger circle and a bigger tribe as a wonderful web of Sistership Circles, conscious women and divine feminine leaders span across our planet.

I am truly honored and forever grateful. Tanya Lynn is a true modern day Goddess and Heroine, and Sistership Circle is such a beautiful reflection of this.

~ Sharlene Belusevic

Inquiry Journaling/Affirming Rituals

1. Journal your thoughts on where ancient traditions meet with modern culture. How does this intersection of concepts honor who you are, where you came from, and where you are going?

Chapter 9: Healing the Sisterhood Wound

"I am loved, I am seen, I am heard, I am valued, I am supported."

Trust the feminine. Trust the sisterhood. Trust the tribe. Why is this so hard? Because it wasn't safe: cattiness, competition, judgment, being made fun of, teased and put down. Fearing that emotional vulnerability will result in feeling weak and getting hurt. *Trying to fit in. Trying to belong. Wanting so desperately to be loved, seen and heard.*

How about getting excited for a new friendship, wearing your heart on your sleeve and then having it ripped to shreds? So you close up, shut down, and hide, vowing never to open up your heart again.

We were trained in school as small children to keep quiet to fit in. "Don't raise your hand in fear of saying the wrong thing and being criticized." "Don't speak up in fear of being ostracized." "Don't be weird in fear of being bullied." It was all about kids interacting with each other on the surface level, craving to go deeper yet so afraid. The outcome: gossip; distractions; drugs; alcohol.

The sisterhood destroyed. The brotherhood destroyed. No one has my back. I'm not supported. I can't trust. Backstabbed. Thrown under the bus. The crowd will turn against me and I'll be all alone if I speak up, express myself, and tell the truth. *So I'll stifle my self-expression, not let anyone see the real me.*

Fuck my intuition. Screw my gut. I can't trust. I've got to be smart. I've got to use my head, figure out a strategy to stay safe, stay in the tribe and not get kicked out and abandoned.

The sisterhood becomes the sorority. The brotherhood becomes the fraternity. Apply. Put on your A game. Play by the rules. Don't show your vulnerabilities or weaknesses, otherwise they will use it against you. The initiation is how much you are willing to be dominated, bow down to submission ... Not equal. Definitely not safe. But then at least you belong to something.

And we all want to belong. I hated the cheerleading squad. I hated the sororities. I hated the clique. Yet I started the clique, I started many cliques, exiting just as quickly. It was a way of being in control. If I started it, they couldn't exclude me. I leave so you can't kick me out. I've got it covered.

Deep down, I craved deeper intimacy, loyalty, integrity, and accountability. Will you be all in? Will you do whatever it takes? How far can I push you, test your commitment?

This is from a closed down, broken heart. Protecting myself from getting hurt. Again. And time and time again, I've sought out solace with the masculine.

The masculine can protect me. I ditch the sisterhood over and over again for the boyfriend. I hide out in my romantic relationship to avoid the feminine. Because I feel loved. I feel wanted and desired. The man has got my back, even if it is temporary. Boyfriends show up differently than women friends; I gravitate toward them because of the masculine strength and sturdy container that I crave. I'm tired of being the masculine and I want to be taken care of. Men provide me what I need.

What Do Women Provide Me?

Can I be friends with someone simply because I like them? Or do I need to need something from them? Does it need to be reciprocal? I kept attracting "needy" women, which keeps me in the cycle of playing the martyr and the savior role in my friendships. And so my relationships with women have been co-dependent and completely draining.

What's your hidden agenda?
Will you leave once you get what you need from me?
Am I really important to you? Or am I second choice?

I could be a victim. I could play the blame and shame game. I could continue to live in my story that I'm unsupported and mistrust the sisterhood. Or I could open my heart a little wider and lean in. Trust the feminine despite feeling burned. Get back to the truth that the sisterhood is a reflection of *me*.

Get back to the fundamentals of Co-Creative Leadership as the high priestess. Taking personal responsibility. Connecting back with my power. Opening myself up to receive divine guidance. Listening. Finding inspiration. I am reminded that the sisterhood co-creates the space to inspire and empower the masculine. I had forgotten.

I had forgotten who I am as a powerful co-creator with the divine. I had forgotten that the sisterhood reflected back my power in our co-creation. It is time for us to lean back in. It is time to call in the sisterhood despite remembering all the times we were burned, abandoned, backstabbed or hurt. This is what it means to open your heart.

Leaning in requires courage. It requires remembering the story we made up about ourselves that we are not safe and taking the leap anyway. It requires remembering further back in time, before the stories we made up, to who we really are. Faith. Trust. The evidence is against it; we've been beat up numerous times. The pain is still there. Real. The wound deep. Scab ripped open, bleeding.

To heal the wound, lean in.
To heal the wound, take the opposite action: open.
Risk getting hurt again. Expose your heart.

Love heals. Love is the soothing balm on the wound. Love conquers fear. Love happens when we open our hearts wide to receive. What's the thing you don't want me to know about you?

That I am really dark. Scary dark. I have so much anger, hate, depression. I have hurt so many people. I destroy. I sabotage. I take it all down.

But I guess it's because I have so much light. I help so many people. I make massive impact on other people's lives. So if I have that much light, then I have that much darkness.

I have such a hard time accepting this about myself. I don't like this feeling. I don't like my darkness. I feel awful. I hate how I am such a powerful creator and then I can't sustain it. I hate how I don't trust others to take responsibility and be accountable. I can't celebrate the successes because all I see is the failures.

My highs are so high. And my lows are so low. And I feel like something is wrong with me that I have these extremes. I have a hard time accepting myself. I don't want you to know about this dark side of me. I don't want you to see the animal, the monster, the demon. So I hide. I hide.

❦

We all have this thought that *if you really knew me, you'd leave me.* You wouldn't accept me. And that's why we don't accept this part of ourselves. But it's there. It's real. It's alive. It's true. When we show up in this vulnerability, sharing the thing we don't want to share, leaning in to the pain, exposing our pain, opening our heart to potentially get stabbed once again, we are finally seen.

At that moment of recognition of both the humanness and the soul that we all share, we connect. We empathize. We relate. We see and we feel seen. We hear and we feel heard. We love and we feel loved. And in that moment, we heal. We both heal.

One time doesn't erase the past hurts. It doesn't take it away, but it gives us courage to open our hearts once again.

And again. Wider.
And again. Wider.
And again. Wider.
And again. Wider.

Our shoulders move back. We aren't hunched over. Our heads tilt up. Our throat clears. We can speak our truth.

What is the sisterhood?

The sisterhood is exactly this mirror. My sister is me. She hears me, I hear myself. She sees me, I see myself. She loves me, I love myself. She mirrors both my light and my dark. She allows me to accept my darkness because she connects with my vulnerability. She still loves me. It is okay.

The disconnect is that you think the sisterhood is outside of you; but the truth is you are the sisterhood. The sisterhood is not some sorority you need to prove yourself to get into; *the sisterhood lies within your heart.*

Not many women have experienced this type of sisterhood I am speaking to. It is available once we access our hearts. So many women are shocked when they come to Tribal Truth saying it is the most authentic group they had ever experienced. It feels so good. It feels so liberating, so inviting, so loving.

So many women exit as quickly as they enter because of these old patterns. There is an energy that creates the contraction from "yes I want this" to "I'm out of here, this isn't for me, this isn't what I thought it was ..."

What is this thing that constantly pulls us, humanity, apart, thinking we are alone and separate? I believe it is the problem of "specialness."

Every time I am with a group and someone invites another person to something but doesn't extend the invitation to me, I am devastated. I know it is not personal. I know people don't have situational awareness sometimes. But even knowing that, I get hurt every time that I feel excluded or worse, forgotten. Sometimes it triggers livid anger in me. I'm afraid of this feeling and so I keep it to myself.

I've come to recognize that I feel rejected. I feel like I am not "special" to this person that they wouldn't invite me. I am highly sensitive to this because of my role in community of making sure everyone is always included. My ego wants to feel special. My ego feels stepped on.

But I am not special. I am a divine being given unique gifts and talents to be able to serve on earth. But I am not special. Specialness is an illusion. This specialness is what fuels a feeling of belonging. So when we no longer feel special, we no longer feel like we belong; we feel separate.

❦

Pseudocommunity is built on the specialness factor. Who's who. Popularity. Getting ahead by who you know. Pseudocommunity is a term coined by M Scott Peck in his book *The Different Drum* :

The most familiar form of group flight is found in what I have termed "pseudocommunity." The basic assumption of pseudocommunity is that the problem of individual differences should be avoided. The boring mannerliness of pseudocommunity is a pretense devoted to fleeing from anything that might cause healthy as well as unhealthy conflict.[17]

We get all excited to be included in the group where we are superficially connected and any little upset can have us become fair-weather fans and drop out.

Real community erases the specialness factor. Real community occurs when we drop the pretense and we open our hearts and lean in. We are committed no matter what comes up. We don't have the need to "belong" because judgment no longer exists in the space. We've got each other's backs no matter what. The bond is deeper.

The sorority is based on the ego's specialness factor. You are special therefore you belong. The real sisterhood is based on truth and the essence of who we truly are. We are one; therefore, I love you unconditionally because I love myself. It is a soul connection. We are all souls in human form, brought to one another for a reason. The soul mate exists so we can learn our life lessons and continue to grow and expand into more of who we really are, letting go of false pretenses, conditioning and ego.

The ego serves a very specific purpose: to keep us safe, to survive. Interested in thriving beyond survival? Master a deeper level of awareness of yourself, each other and the earth. We coexist. We co-create. We live in symbiotic relationship with one another and the planet. Harmony.

I see the real sisterhood as having a significant role in creating a new culture. It's not about women empowering ourselves and one another in resistance and rebellion from the current wounded masculine structure. It's not about separation but about integration of the masculine and feminine within ourselves.

⁂

What is this deep desire to connect? What is this craving for community that quickly turns into upset and withdrawal? Why do we feel so

What is this deep desire to connect? What is this craving for community that quickly turns into upset and withdrawal? Why do we feel so down and depressed one day and back up the next? Why do we feel like we are different and don't belong?

It comes down to the core wound of "I'm not enough." We each have our own flavor of it and have played out various ways to cover it up, avoid the feelings associated with it, and prove that it is not true.

"I'm Not Enough" is the name of the scary monster hiding in the closet. It wears all the clothing in your closet as masks to hide itself. These masks all help your monster feel liked, appreciated, valued, included, and special. The masks help your monster fit in with all the other masks so you feel like you belong despite feeling like you are the ugliest in the room. It is sneaky. It has you fooled.

The purpose of the tribe is to create a safe space for you to take off the mask and reveal your scary monster. As soon as you put the spotlight on the monster, you suddenly see it's not as scary as you made it out to be. It shrinks, it evaporates, and suddenly, it is no longer lurking in the dark, so you become free to be the truth of who you are.

The tribe acts as a mirror to reflect back at you two things: your darkness and your light. The women show up as their monster, which triggers you because they are mirrors of your own, and this is so you can finally face it within yourself. The women also show up as their truth, which is love and compassion, mirroring your own greatness for you to reclaim and own.

When we see the tribe in this context, a playground where all the monsters and angels come out to horseplay and wrestle, push each other and hug each other, we finally gain the necessary awareness to heal together.

The goal then, is not to force people into tribe if they are not aware of this context and hence not ready for their own healing. The goal, instead, is to focus on the people who are ready to commit and lean in to this process. One by one, each person heals, affecting their inner circles. As one person shifts, the people around her notice and are affected. It is a ripple effect.

This is the feminine at work. The feminine is like a flower that when she blooms, attracts the bees to come and drink her nectar. She doesn't need to do anything. She simply has to be. Allow the process. Shine her light. Be her radiance.

We have an extraordinary opportunity to create a worldwide sisterhood tribe. It starts by looking within at our own individual sacred wound and allowing the medicine of the circle to heal us. As we focus on ourselves, taking personal responsibility for our own stories and wounds, transforming them by letting go of the beliefs while feeling the feelings arising, we turn the illusion of separation into the reality of connection.

Together, we turn hindrances into intimacy.
Turn gossip into asking the source
Turn complaining into celebrating
Turn positioning wars into collaborations
Turn protecting oneself into opening oneself
Turn rejecting first to leaning in first
Turn hardening into softening
Turn fixing, coaching, converting, and changing (under guise of speaking truth) into listening
Turn holding grudges into forgiveness
Turn blame, shame, and guilt into truth telling
Turn forcing into allowing
Turn competition into cooperation
Turn projections into reflections
Turn not feeling supported into asking for support.

So many women around the world are gathering in circles over the past few years with the rise of the feminine. It is time to merge. How? We stop creating separation based on interests and purpose of gathering and start looking to build diversity. Diversity brings richness, depth and creativity. Acknowledging and celebrating diversity is what will stop the fighting on our planet. There is no "better than" or "less than," simply a difference in perspective. When we can start to recognize that we all come from different backgrounds, even within the same town, and that we have something to learn from one another, we can start to piece together these separate tribes into one common tribe nation.

Creating world peace starts with sisterhood tribes merging, collaborating, cooperating, and co-creating. It starts with women honoring each woman's ancestral lineage and celebrating the wisdom that has been passed down to her. It starts with honoring that each one of us has something to teach one another; that each one of us has something to learn from one another.

No more "what's in it for me?" Instead we ask, "What can I give? How can I serve my sisters and humanity?" No more pyramids, putting one person on a pedestal. The sisterhood is a circle of equals, rich in diversity, abundant with wisdom.

The masculine competes. The feminine collaborates. This is the way for our future. *This is how we will create world peace.*

This is why I teach and provide a framework for Circle Work, so that women leaders can gather the women in their community. You can use Sistership Circle's teachings to create your own tribe or enhance one you are already a part of. Get the 7 Principles to Lead Circle at: http:// SistershipCircle.com/eBook.

Sister Spotlight: Kelly's Story

Sistership Circle showed up during a time in my life when I needed it most. I had finally seen the completion of a long and difficult divorce, and had just moved to a new city after living in the Bay Area my entire life. If that wasn't enough change, I had also just started a brand new job.

I was fortunate enough to have known Tanya and the brilliant work she was doing, but I didn't quite know what I was getting myself into when I said "yes" to her invitation to join Sistership. Up until that point, I had been feeling shunned by several of my friends. It was as if they didn't know how or worse yet, didn't want to support me through my divorce.

Interestingly, I felt myself holding back and not fully expressing the depth of my sorrow, grief and depression with the few friends that stayed by my side. I feared that I would drive them away, too, because I lacked faith in the bond of true sisters. I had become accustomed to showing up only partially real, because deep down I felt that if people really knew how I was feeling and what I was thinking, they would run the other way.

I learned this in school with girlfriends who I considered my best friends. I was shunned too many times by girls who were more concerned about what other's thought about them than by being true to a friend. That sting stayed with me for decades.

I was feeling very alone and lonely when I showed up for Sistership Circle. It had been a very long and painful couple of years. I wasn't sure what to expect but having known Tanya for a few years prior to circle, I felt safe in knowing that she would hold sacred space for me and the other women who showed up.

Something told me this experience would be different. Something told me that if only I could learn to trust myself enough to be real in the presence of other women, my life might change for the better.

I was nervous and excited all at the same time that first night. I didn't even know if I would "get along" with the other women in circle. They were complete strangers to me and yet something about them seemed familiar.

Friendships in the past weren't always based on unconditional love and feeling held by the other. Often times there was a sense of competition and times when I felt betrayed by those that I thought were supposed to have my back. This experience was completely different.

The women who sat in circle with me were all there for the same reason – to be seen, to be held, to speak her truth and to hold space for her circle sisters.

It didn't happen right away, but eventually I learned to trust that no matter what I said or did, I wasn't being judged. I was only shown compassion and love. Seeing this time and again, I began showing up to circle in ways I had never done before. Pouring out my heart, being real and raw with my emotions became the norm.

I didn't realize how guarded I was with my deepest fears and even my wildest dreams before I joined circle. There, I found a place where I could show up just as I was whether it was bright and shiny, or dark and gloomy. No matter what, I felt loved and held by the most amazing women.

Sistership Circle was so completely transformative for me that I continued to join Tanya's next level circles and every time I grew even more. I am so grateful to have followed my heart to take the leap of faith that allowed me to trust in feminine leadership and in the power of co-creation. It is truly one of the best gifts I've given myself and it just keeps giving.

~ Kelly A Greene

Inquiry Journaling/Affirming Rituals

1. What is your wound around the sacred feminine?

2. What experiences of cattiness, competition and comparison have you encountered with other girls/women?

Chapter 10: Weaving the Three C's of Tribe

"I'm leaning in."

"Until one is committed, there is hesitancy, the chance to draw back —
Concerning all acts of initiative (and creation), there is one elementary
truth that ignorance of which kills countless ideas and splendid plans: that
the moment one definitely commits oneself, then Providence moves too. All
sorts of things occur to help one that would never otherwise have occurred.
A whole stream of events issues from the decision, raising in one's favor all
manner of unforeseen incidents and meetings and material assistance, which
no man could have dreamed would have come his way. Whatever you can do,
or dream you can do, begin it. Boldness has genius, power, and magic in it.
Begin it now." ~ W.H. Murrary, from The Scottish Himalayan Expedition

There are many threads that weave together a tribe, but if I had to
distill it down to the main three, it would come down to *commitment,*
connection and communication. These are the tenets to create a safe space
for people to come together and be vulnerable and authentic with one
another.

Commitment

It always starts with a commitment, which ultimately means taking
the action to show up.

Why is it so hard for people to commit?

We want our options open; there may be something better over there. The grass is always greener on the other side.

We want to make sure we have the time and energy for something we commit to. We don't want to burn ourselves out. We say we want to be able to give it our all.

We want to discern so that what we are committing to feels aligned with our other commitments. It has to feel good, feed our heart and soul, and serve or contribute to our purpose.

We want to make sure we trust, like and know the other people who we are in the commitment with.

We want to have confirmation that we made the right choice.

We want to feel safe.

We want to gain value.

These concerns are all valid and appropriate things to consider before making any commitment. But what if I said that this all prevents you from actually connecting in the way that I am describing? What if I asked you to let all of those concerns go and open your heart to a new possibility? All of these concerns come from fear, scarcity and separation. These concerns are what actually deter us from creating the type of tribe nation I am talking about.

Here's the tribe dilemma. We say we want world peace and yet we are constantly judging and assessing people and communities, putting each tribe into a category of good, bad or neutral, creating factions and separation. And yet, this is an absolutely critical part of living in a dualistic worldview where right and wrong, masculine and feminine, light and dark, separation and connection exist. Discernment, boundaries, and limitations exist. So let's call a spade a spade and say that until we come to the realization that there is no right or wrong, we will continue to be in this paradigm that we so desperately want to escape.

To come to this place of seeing reality as it is, we must heal this divide within ourselves and see ourselves as whole. This should really be the only thing to look at when committing to tribe: I am committing to healing myself with the mirror reflections of my tribe. I am really only committing to myself.

Date: _____

I commit to my learning, growth and expansion.

I commit to feeling unconditionally.

I commit to leaning in when I want to run away from myself.

I commit to facing myself.

I commit to showing up exactly as I am.

I commit to be gentle with myself.

I commit to self-love.

I commit to self-acceptance.

I commit to let go of judging myself, fixing myself, changing myself and making myself wrong.

I commit to tell the truth to myself and others.

I commit to opening my heart when I feel like shutting down.

I commit to me.

I commit to tribe.

Signed, _____

Download this printable commitment form
at sistershipcircle.com/downloads

To commit fully, you must surrender because there will be ups and downs, highs and lows. It will not be an easy ride. But in the commitment comes the growth. In the commitment comes safety to let go and be yourself.

It is a risk because it is foreign and unknown. This type of sisterhood does not exist in the mainstream. Mean Girls exists in the mainstream. But this is what we all want, our heart's desire. With the biggest risks come the greatest returns.

Connection

The greatest connection occurs when two people who meet are both connecting to themselves. When two people meet and are distracted, thinking about what else they need to do and where else they need to be, a connection cannot exist. Therefore, we must learn to be fully present.

I have learned a trick to help me do this. Whenever I meet someone and they ask me, "how are you?" I actually check in with myself. I pause and do a quick body scan. Is there any tension in my body? Is there any feeling that stands out in an area of my body? Is there any thought associated with that feeling?

Instead of giving the standard, "I'm great!" or "I'm fine," I get present to my body and my feelings. When I am present, I can establish a deeper connection with the human being in front of me.

When I am present, I have a new perspective on the world. I see that the universe is giving me exactly what I need in every given moment. So instead of seeing this person in front of me and looking around to see who else is around, I can see this person as exactly the person I'm supposed to talk to in that moment. This lends itself to deeper connection.

This person may have a job lead if I am looking for employment, a connection if I'm looking for a new client, or a dog sitter if I'm going out of town next week.

This person is suddenly my new best friend in that moment. My biggest opportunity. My greatest ally. My genie in a bottle. Think about this … how cool is that for you to be someone's genie in a bottle? That you are that powerful to grant them their wish.

We aren't always present, especially when we have so much to do, so many thoughts racing through our minds, and so many distractions in this crazy, busy world we live in. So whenever people gather in a group, the absolute first necessary step is to establish a connection. Forget agendas, outlines, goals and timelines.

Connect. Without setting this foundational piece, the tribe will fall apart and may never come back together again. People carry so much baggage with them, most of the time hidden from view. Here are the steps that we have taken to establish that connection:

1) **Breathe**. Get people out of their heads and into their bodies by connecting with their breath. Once they are breathing, they can then do a body scan to see what they are feeling.

2) **Feel**. Each sensation in the body is related to a thought, which is tied to an emotion. Instead of suppressing these thoughts and emotions, the point here is to feel them unconditionally. Allow them to be. Stop trying to pretend everything is fine and dandy when there is something that wants to be expressed.

3) **Permission**. We have been trained to ask for permission in school and from our parents, and so most people need permission to be vulnerable.

4) **Safety**. Create safe space by getting a white board and writing down on the board what makes people feel unsafe and what makes them feel safe. Set ground rules so that people feel like they can be vulnerable.

Sample ground rules:
- No judgment, criticism or put downs.
- No coaching, fixing or giving someone advice unless they ask for it.
- Confidentiality.

- Active listening. Honor someone by giving your attention when someone is speaking.

5) **Leadership**. Set the tone by being vulnerable, real and authentic. Share your feelings. This means you, whether or not you are the designated leader of the group.

6) **Clear**. Put two people together in paired shares to share about anything that is in their heads. The point here is to empty out everything that may be in the way of being present. This could include sharing about what may have happened during the day or right before arriving. The point is not to get caught in the story, but to let it go.

7) **Create**. Set an intention for the time spent together in tribe. Express gratitude for being here. Make a choice to be fully present. Remember, how can you be a genie in the bottle for someone if you are not present?

Women have expressed to me that the way they feel safe is by connecting, and the way they feel connected is by sharing. It takes just a few minutes for women to open up and start talking to one another. To facilitate this, women need both the individual and group connection. When I lead a tribe gathering, I ask women to find five women to connect with one on one and then I put everyone in a circle to share their name and one thing they want the group to know about them.

The most important question to ask the group is: "Is anyone holding onto something that will prevent them from being present?" The more authentic the connection, the closer the tribe feels to one another. Authentic connection happens when people have the space to be real and express their feelings.

The trick here is in not reacting to people's feelings. I have found time and time again that people need space to empty out and then it disappears. There is nothing to do with what they said, simply hold the space for it to be. When we accept what is, allowing it to be, it disappears. Just like watching an itch instead of reacting to it ... eventually it will go away.

Communication

Communication is essential to maintaining the ongoing connection. Stuff is going to come up. Triggers. Fear. Upsets. Communication is the key to answering two of the pivotal questions we asked at the beginning of this book:

> *How do we create community that sticks together through thick and thin?*
> *How do we handle our upsets and frustrations with one another when they come up?*

Withholds

Why do we withhold the truth? We have bought into the beliefs that ...

You can't handle it
I don't want to hurt you
I have shame and guilt
You have no appreciation
Need to know basis
Confidential
It will cause disruption and disharmony
You'll abandon me
It's ugly and I don't want to be responsible
My fear of judgment
I'll get in trouble
You'll compete with me.

The biggest threat to a tribe's foundation is withholds.

Withholds can be anything we have not communicated to another person or persons. Withholds are un-communicated charges, or energy – both positive and negative – that exist between us and another person. When appropriately delivered, this communication tool results in reducing the charge, making it possible for a much greater level of affinity and love between oneself and another. Withholds are a way for us to be responsible for our own charge while giving ourselves more freedom in relationship to people we care about. This tool is also a powerful way to empty our minds so that we can simply be more present in life.

Example:

Person A: There's something I've withheld from you.
Person B: OK, would you like to tell me.
Person A: I got really upset with the way you told me to take my seat.
Person B: Thank you.

Note the following:

1. While delivering a withhold, the person communicating is free to express any and all emotions.

2. The person receiving a withhold must remain completely neutral to create safety for the person communicating.

3. The content of withholds does not get discussed at a later point in time unless a clear agreement exists between the two people.

4. When an extremely high charge exists between two people, we recommend that a third party hold space for this process. Do not deliver your withholds directly to the person with whom you have the charge. It is too easy to want to "clobber" that person. Remember, you're doing withholds to avoid that type of reaction!

Permission to Tell the Truth

What I want the most in the world is to be able to speak my truth freely. I want that knot in my stomach to go away that says, "Don't say it! You'll be in trouble! You will regret it as soon as it comes out of your mouth!" I want to be able to say anything to anyone at any time anywhere.

I don't want to live in fear of judgment. I am committed to embody my full expression. And I want to be grounded in my knowing that what I am saying is in the highest good, that I do not intend to cause harm, that my truth is spoken to create connection.

As I've committed to this path of truth seeking and truth telling, I've recognized how much I avoid speaking the truth in fear of abandonment and judgment.

I've also recognized that the more I feel, the less I get hijacked by the fear. The more I speak the truth, the more I receive the affirmation that I am safe. That knot in my stomach dissipates. Yes, speaking the truth is getting easier. I keep pushing the edge of my vulnerability further and further out, allowing all parts of myself to be seen.

There is really nothing for me to hide. I'm not about saying "the right thing" so you'll buy something from me. I'm not about saying "the good thing" to make you feel better.

Of course, what runs in the background is that I want everyone to like me, to feel accepted and to feel included. So of course I have trepidation around speaking up and screwing up.

But as a leader, I have to recognize that when people don't like me, that's their stuff getting triggered. I cannot be responsible for your reactions. And I get so responsible. I want so badly to fix it. I become obsessed. My job is to let go and let you go through *your* process.

Reflecting on triggers and the impact of stifling your truth is amazing – it leads to discovering the "story" that runs in the background of our minds. An example came to me as I sat on my meditation mat one day. I had this visual memory come to my mind of my father turning around and smacking me in the backseat. I don't know what I was doing. Probably talking back, trying to get the last word, fighting with my brother. In that moment, I fumed. I raged internally. I clenched my teeth and clamped my mouth shut because I didn't dare speak the feelings that bubbled up beneath the surface. It wasn't safe, I thought, for me to speak up.

I continued to stifle my truth, holding onto the admonition that "if you speak up you'll be in trouble" and "what you have to say doesn't matter" and "expect to be a scapegoat" and "feel guilty for antagonizing others."

My reaction was to scream, "Fuck you I'm out of here!" But I kept my mouth shut and being trapped in that car, I checked out. Nowhere to go. Not safe to speak. Suffer in silence.

And again and again, I would stick around in relationships that would mirror my relationship with my father ... they'd break up with me, they'd leave me, they'd check out. Boyfriends. Friends. Colleagues. Clients.

You may want to bail out of a relationship because it triggers a past feeling that you don't want to feel. The triggers come up for a reason: for you to fully feel what's coming up and clear the story that keeps running your life.

Triggers

All we have is relationship otherwise we'd live in a vacuum. And relationship is defined by how we relate to one another. Each moment, we have a choice of how to relate. Relationships are so hard because we typically relate to one another from the past, either from our individual past or from our relationship in the past. We have a hard time starting fresh with no expectations, assumptions, or triggers.

We are usually comparing and judging. We struggle to stay in the present moment in our relationships because one thing will remind us of the past and we've been conditioned to react in a certain way to protect ourselves from getting hurt again.

If you notice, you tend to have the same pattern happen over and over again in each relationship. The same need doesn't get met, the same fight happens, the same words used, the same feeling triggered.

Why do we keep having the same fight? Why do I feel like a hamster on a wheel? Why does nothing change? Until you can solve the underlying root issue, you will continue to bring the same problem from relationship to relationship until you get it.

It will continue to reappear and the typical response is: "I'm tired of attracting the same dirt-bag guy" or "Why do I feel so unsupported by my friends?" or "My friend is so self-centered" instead of looking within. Remember, when pointing the finger out there, three fingers are pointing back at yourself.

You are at the source, you are the common denominator. There is no one else out there. Relationships are a mirror reflection of you. Whatever shows up provides you the opportunity to heal.

Have you noticed how many people piss you off? Have you noticed how many times you turn against your community? It's because they trigger you. To trigger is to initiate, actuate, or set off; to cause the explosion of. It is no coincidence when someone says something that frustrates, annoys or bothers you, because they are triggering an emotional response to an old wound; *there are chemicals being set off in reaction to the wound.*

It is not the perpetrator. It's not anything to do with the person in front of you. That person is simply triggering your own response to the action. The person in the present moment is just doing what he normally does, being him. You are the one with the emotional reaction. So it's time to do some work so that the trigger no longer has an effect on you. No more explosion.

Releasing the Trigger

What are the biggest issues in your relationships? The best way to identify them is by looking at the things you complain about, which are essentially the admonitions from your childhood.

No one invites me anywhere. I'm the last to find out.

I'm always excluded.

I don't fit in.

I'm jealous of her.

Why does no one call me?

I feel so unsupported.

I try and it's not reciprocated.

When I ask for what I want, I get rejected.

I don't want to be a bother.

I feel like I'm in the way.

I always have to do it his way.

It's all about him.

The root is always coming from "I'm not enough, therefore you will x." What's your x? What's your biggest fear? What's the worse that they would do to you?

Abandon me

Dislike me

Judge me

Disown me

Criticize me

We protect ourselves from experiencing this deepest pain. How do you protect yourself?

Run away

Avoid

Hold back

Charm

Put down

Where has this trigger shown up in the past? What's the thread that you can trace back in time in your relationships? When we are triggered, there is a story attached, but we feel like we are in our truth. So what is my truth? I hear from people, "… but this is my truth." My question in return is: "Is it really?"

In the moment, it is your experience. It is your perception, but is it your truth really? The truth, in this case, is the essence. The truth is what remains when all else falls away. The truth, for me, is in love.

Which means I allow it.
I give myself permission.
I stop being hard on myself.
I forgive and accept myself.
I show up in every moment alive and present.
I lean into relationships.
I create an environment of vulnerability.
I take care of myself.
I have meaningful conversations.
I give generously.
I open my heart to receive.
I clear and release.
I express gratitude.
I feel all of it.
I unconditionally love myself.
I see the beauty all around me, even in the things that look and smell bad.
I see the perfect divine timing of everything.
I feel the Presence of God within my heart and all around me.
I maintain my daily practice of meditation and breathwork.

My relationship to you is powerful because you are always my mirror. I get to see my fullness, each aspect of myself in you. I get to see the parts I don't like and do like and all are valid and all equally important. I get to learn how to accept myself because of you. Thank you. I am grateful for you. You are paramount to my survival, my evolution, and my freedom. Without you, nothing is possible. With you, anything is possible.

Sister Spotlight: Lori's Story

I came into this world a very quiet, introspective, sensitive child. Looking back, I realize I never felt like I deserved to be here. To prove my worthiness, I did everything I could for anyone and everyone but myself. I became the ultimate people pleaser, the good girl. I thought that if I was quiet enough, behaved myself, got good grades, had a successful career and didn't ask for much, then I would deserve to be here and I would find the connection I so desperately longed for. Maybe if I hid in the shadows, no one would notice me and I could stay awhile.

People in my life echoed my belief that I didn't deserve to be here. Just before my 4th birthday, my paternal grandmother said she was going to visit my (much older) sister and her family. Intuitively I knew this meant she wouldn't be present for my birthday, and I spoke up about it. Her response was "that doesn't matter." Proof to my tiny self that I didn't matter. Proof that I should remain quiet.

As the years went by, I encountered more evidence that I didn't matter, that I didn't deserve to be here. So I worked harder – in school and later in my career - thinking if I just *did enough*, then I would be worthy of life. I did everything I could to not be a burden on anyone and became hyper independent. I was always on alert for any way I might have let someone down so I could quickly make up for it, thereby earning my right to be here. Earning my right *to be*.

In doing so, I often isolated myself. I was afraid if anyone got too close, they would learn my hidden secret, that I didn't deserve to be here. They would find out I was a fraud. So while I had a few close friends, I never let anyone very close to me. The connection I wanted eluded me, especially the connection to myself and to my soul. I disconnected from my body and stayed up in my head. It was safe there.

I didn't let anyone know what I wanted, because I was afraid that if I did, they would laugh at me. Or respond like my grandmother had all those years before and reject me. Or worse yet, they would leave me. So I stuffed down every desire, every feeling, every opinion, every emotion, every part of me. In doing so, I abandoned myself. I didn't think I had anything to share that mattered. I lost my voice.

All of this cost me more than one marriage, because I never truly committed to anyone, most importantly myself. It cost me a relationship that likely would have led to a marriage I did deserve, that I've always wanted. Instead, I settled for less than what I truly desired, not thinking I was worthy.

Until I could no longer do any of that. Until I could no longer hide. Until I could no longer stay silent. Until I could no longer abandon myself.

It began slowly, as many awakenings do. The sleepless nights. The feeling of being stifled and unfulfilled in my career and marriage. The yearning from a place deep inside that I was disconnected from.

I started seeking, not even knowing what I was seeking. I made new choices, from a new place. From a deep knowing that I came to this life for more than what I was living. I was on a quest to find myself, my soul, my very reason for being in this life.

I was shocked when I realized that my intuition is very strong – I had just ignored it most of my life, listening instead to the mental chatter in my head. Once I started listening to my intuition and following it, I found so much of what I'd always wanted.

At the age of 47, I left my third and last marriage. At 50, I started my own business, which was a huge leap for me after working for others my entire life.

In the searching, I found joy again. I found the beauty in connecting with myself in the stillness, and in community with other women. I said yes to myself and to life in a way I'd always wanted to, but hadn't felt I deserved. I found my voice, and I learned to share it. In my sharing, I began to find my tribe.

Along the way, I became a member of Sistership Circle. There was something about Tanya's community that called to me, and I knew I wanted that connection with other women. In this community I have shared pieces of myself that I had been afraid to share. In doing so, I have been seen, heard, and honored for who I am as a woman - not rejected, laughed at, or abandoned as I'd always feared. It has allowed me to step up in my life and business as a true leader, leading from my heart.

Along with working with women privately, I now lead my own circles of women, Awaken the Woman Within Sacred Women's Circle, offering women the experience of connecting with themselves and other women, of sharing even when they're afraid to share, and of celebrating the beauty of life and the feminine.

I now know what I desire in this life, and I express it. I have committed to myself at a whole new level. I take exquisite care of myself so I am able to better serve others in my life. I connect deeply with other women who are doing the same.

As a symbol of the commitment I've made to myself, I recently got my first tattoo. On the inside of my left wrist is inscribed the word "Truth." It's a reminder of the commitment I've made to myself to always speak my truth from an open heart, with grace, compassion and kindness.

~ Lori Latimer

Inquiry Journaling/Affirming Rituals

1. Journal about a relationship that is stressed or suffering because of a trigger you are holding onto. What is the "story" running in the background? Will you let it go? How can you reframe it?

Chapter 11: Sustain the Movement

"I surrender."

During the first section of this book, we dove into what makes you, the individual woman, alive: stepping into your leadership and loving yourself as a high priestess; letting go, accepting and forgiving; sustaining your personal energy through self-care; expressing your essence through your sexuality; and owning your worth so you can live prosperously. These are specific areas of growth and expansion that translate directly to the sustainability of the tribe. The more that you are grounded and solid in your own sustainability, the more the tribe will be a direct reflection of that.

The cracks in your foundation as a woman affect the container of the tribe. There is no *us versus them*. There is no tribe outside of ourselves. *We* are the tribe. *You* are the tribe.

If we want to create a sustainable society where we live in harmony with the earth, it starts with the individual, trickles into how we relate to one another in our communities, and then ripples out to the rest of the world.

Tribal Truth/Sistership Circle has been a science experiment, a study of sisterhood. We've identified the seven biggest obstacles and ten foundational pillars to sustaining tribe.

The Seven Biggest Obstacles to Sustaining Tribe
#1: Bottleneck Leadership

A movement needs a charismatic, dynamic leader. Someone who has a clear vision, confidence in herself and a capacity to hold the vision long term. She cannot get trapped in fear and self-doubt.

She must trust herself, her team and God's way.
She must keep her feelings out of it and take nothing personal.
And most importantly: she must get out of the frickin' way.

If the leader cannot empower and then trust others to take on responsibility, she becomes a bottleneck. Micromanagement cannot exist in a tribe. If you think of the leader like the brain of a human, you can see that while it is absolutely critical to survival, the heart and other organs are vital, too. Strong body, mind, spirit *and* heart.

Too many leaders get stuck making it about them. They think that the tribe cannot exist without their leadership. In a Co-Creative Leadership tribe, the focus is not on one individual taking care of the rest, but instead everyone taking shared responsibility. The leader must let go of control in order for this to happen. The leader must empower and inspire people from the onset to take on their accountability.

#2: Money Floats to the Top

If people pay for a membership to a tribe, they expect to get something in return. The exchange is money for a service, which has a perceived value.

As soon as money is involved, the members are expecting someone to do something for them. They do not see themselves as equal owners of the tribe.

In Co-Creative Leadership, everyone must see themselves as an equal spoke in the wheel with ownership of the wheel.

But why not create a profit-based model where all of the members can benefit? Tribe does not have to mean non-profit or free, especially in a world where currency, not barter or a free market, exists. If the tribe were to take on a profit-based model, I propose the following:

1. Membership based: Every member pays monthly, quarterly or annual dues. Members then are encouraged to expand the tribe by receiving a percentage of membership dues of every new member they refer.

2. The tribe participates in a shared revenue, or dividend, model creating a product or service outside of itself. All members have ownership like stockholders. Every tribe member has a specific role or accountability. The tribe agrees unanimously upon the value of those specific roles and accountabilities.

3. If there is personal development or business training events put on by the leader or another member, members pay for those services, just as they would normally. Same goes for coaching or other programs.

#3: Expectations, Agreements and Boundaries

Culture is based on shared values, language, beliefs and rituals. Tribes create their own culture ... that's what makes them stick. What people are looking for is to opt out of a culture based on fear and greed and instead participate in a culture based on love that values people, planet and profits equally.

This is the culture that Co-Creative Leadership creates.

Questions around boundaries come up: is this tribe closed to certain members? Should people apply? What would happen if the doors are wide open for anyone? What if someone is disruptive and abusive to others in the tribe? How do we handle discipline?

There is a difference between boundaries and barriers, which Danielle LaPorte describes as such:

Boundaries are like a fence with a gate—the energy can come and go. You know you're protected. Boundaries say, this works for me, this doesn't.

And because you've made those clear declarations—about your standards— then you can be at peace within your gate. You can chill because you have told the world how you prefer to be treated.

Barriers are like a shield that you drag around—ready to defend yourself from attacks.

It's not very peaceful. Being on guard all the time is anxiety-inducing.

As soon as we begin to create barriers, we are essentially putting a new mask on the old paradigm that we are running away from. This is not a "new paradigm," but an alternative to the mainstream paradigm. As more people opt-out of the old paradigm, it starts to become the new mainstream. Look at Whole Foods and the organic industry: supposedly better, but now turning into a conglomerate, corporate structure that needs to fudge its own rules to keep up with the demand. Suddenly, the restrictions and standards are lowered and it looks like another version of the thing it was trying to be a solution to.

To create barriers is to create separation. To create barriers is to continue the model that we want to opt-out of. And yet we need healthy boundaries to honor the individual *and* the collective.

The intention behind setting expectations, agreements and boundaries is not to limit, exclude or separate, but to create a container within which we can create deeper, more authentic connection. We create safety, trust and commitment.

Some of the questions to ask when creating agreements:

1. How do we create a container where each woman feels loved, seen, heard and valued?
2. How do we lovingly and compassionately call each other out on story and sabotaging beliefs?
3. How do we provide an intimate environment for vulnerable sharing (this does not have to do with size of the group, but energy of the group)?
4. How do we work through our differences and stay together through thick and thin?

5. How do we handle upsets, fights and disagreements?
6. How do we ensure equal participation and ownership?
7. How do we take care of people when they are in breakdown?
8. How do we communicate with one another?

#4: Withholds – Unspoken Judgments, Unresolved Fights, and Gossip

The number one obstacle to keeping a tribe together is **withholds** that build up and then reach a tipping point where the tribe implodes. Withholds are the antithesis of authenticity. They get in the way of connection. They destroy friendships. They prevent you from being present. They are the destruction of tribe.

We are constantly walking around judging and assessing; it's part of human nature. However, if we hold onto these judgments against the people in our circle, then we are not relating to them as who they are anymore, but who we make them up to be.

I'm always amazed at how much I make up in my head about someone, and then feel so silly when I share it out loud because it's not true. And that's the point: withholds become monsters in our head that as soon as we shed light on, no longer seem so ugly and scary.

Countless women leave their circle because of a withhold, either a judgment toward another woman in the circle or the circle itself.

One of the biggest fears of being part of a tribe is getting into a fight. Then what? Who leaves? How does it get resolved? We had two women who called off their business partnership and ended their friendship while in the tribe. Instead of taking sides, we honored each woman, hearing both of their sides of the story. Even in a break up, you can lean in and get things complete. We created the Completion Ceremony ritual to help facilitate this process.

In our society, it is more common to go your separate ways either quietly or with a big fight, but rarely do we see conscious, loving completion to relationships. Completion may be one of the most important parts of a relationship, and yet most relationships end with loose ends. A Completion Ceremony is where a woman who decides to leave the tribe receives a ceremony from the tribe. She gets to say anything that is left incomplete and the tribe gets to speak as well. Incompletions include both upsets and acknowledgments. I like to use completion ceremonies for the ending of individual relationships so both people can continue to be in the tribe instead of feeling ostracized.

#5: Fear of Vulnerability

Vulnerability is what has us connect on a deeper level, and yet most people "hang out" on the superficial level, talking about the weather, their favorite food and sports team.

As children, our emotions completely overwhelmed us and so as adults, we have not matured emotionally to feel like we've expanded our capacity to unconditionally feel the grief, anger and fear so we suppress these feelings. Being vulnerable brings up these feelings that we don't want to feel. So it is easier to stay at the superficial level. We don't want to cry because it gets messy and ugly. We don't want someone to see us get upset because we don't want her to judge us. We don't want to fall apart because if we are weak someone may take advantage of us. But underneath all of those fears, we desperately want to be seen. We want people to truly know us. We want people to relate to us. And ironically, the thing we don't want to do is the way to create that deeper connection. Intimacy is when we allow someone to get closer to our true self: "into me see."

So how do we do it? How do we start to see vulnerability as our greatest strength instead of our weakness?

Vulnerability is on a sliding scale. The more I share vulnerably, the less I feel like it is vulnerable. My edge keeps getting pushed further and further out. Suddenly, my capacity expands. I start to mature emotionally, feeling unconditionally, allowing myself to cry in public.

How many times have you seen someone stand up to start sharing something and you feel like she is being so fake? She looks like an actress putting on a terrible show. How many times have you stood up to share something just to look good, covering up how you were really feeling? This is the seed of pseudo-community, a group of individuals coming together to have a good time under the pretence of liking each other and not talking about how they really feel. This type of tribe falls apart as quickly as it started like a fad.

But I don't want to be down and depressed, you may argue. I don't want to talk about my feelings all day long. I want to *feel* good. I want to laugh and have fun with the tribe.

It's only through the darkness that we reach the light. The two cannot exist without each other. Even in the Alaskan summer darkness comes for an hour or two. The objective is not to stay in the shadow, but to shed light on it so it disappears.

The intention is to have an authentic celebration, to truly feel free, not laugh to cover up the feelings underneath.

#6: Weak Facilitation & Container

When I started Tribal Truth, I had coach training and experience leading groups of people, but I did not have the capacity to hold a solid, long-term container for vulnerable, authentic connection. I had to first learn how to be vulnerable and deepen into intimacy with the women around me before I could start to hold that space for others. I had to allow myself to fall apart to become a stronger, more authentic leader.

The container is only as strong as its holder. The facilitator must be able to read the room. She must trust her intuition and if she feels anything in her body that doesn't feel "right," she must trust it and speak up. She must scan people's body language and make sure she says the appropriate thing for them to relax, loosen up and feel safe. She must be in her body at all times. She must make adjustments to her agenda according to the mood and energy in the room. This is what it means to "hold space."

You cannot learn how to hold space from a book; it is something you learn over time from experience. You learn from trial and error. You start to notice when you should speak up and when you should stay silent and listen. There is tremendous power in *listening for something*. If there is an argument in the room, I start to notice within my own body how I am feeling and let go of my own tension. I then notice any judgments I have and let them go. I start to listen for an intended outcome: in this case of an argument, I start to think about both people starting to listen to one another instead of trying to be right. I intend for them to come to that realization on their own. Nine times out of ten, they do. I don't always have to speak up to facilitate a room. Sometimes, as soon as I start speaking up, I add more fuel to the fire, making it worse.

#7: Lack of Leadership Training

If everyone relies on one person to lead, what happens when that person gets sick or even dies? The tribe dies. The tribe cannot be based on one leader. Everyone is constantly changing, growing and evolving and so is every tribe. It makes sense then, that just like going through different levels of education, everyone in a tribe expands their capacity to lead. We are all leaders in our own way. Our job is to keep growing.

In most cultures, boys and girls went through a rite of passage from childhood to adulthood. Why don't we have this in our culture today? What happened to mentorship in helping boys become men and girls become women, stepping over the threshold into adulthood?

The same goes for leadership. As we grow wiser and more mature, it is natural that we start to teach and mentor those who are at the beginning stages. A critical aspect of tribe is mentorship and rites of passage. This is how we sustain to have multiple generations exist together with the elders mentoring and guiding the young.

A friend of mine once told me that he had this vision and didn't know what to do with it except my name came to mind so he thought he'd pass it along and see if I could do something with it.

"I saw this vision of twelve elder women sitting in a circle making decisions for the community. I saw this on the local, state and national levels," he said.

Not only is this vision powerful in honoring the wisdom of the crone, or elder woman, but also demonstrates what could be possible when leadership comes from a circle and not a hierarchy.

Co-Creative Leadership Wheel in Action

The concept of Co-Creative Leadership starts with you, the individual, co-creating with the divine. You are powerful. You are a creator. You are worthy. You are like a unique snowflake, one of a kind. Knowing this about yourself, you own your gifts, talents and knowledge. You know what you have to offer the world.

Most people do not know their place in the world. They don't own their unique gifts and talents. They feel inadequate as if just doing one thing really well is not enough. So they try to be everything to all people. They try to do it all. Let this go.

If you need support in identifying your gifts and strengths, I highly recommend Strength Finder. [18] When you buy the book, you are given a code to go to the website and take the test. This is a brilliant way for tribes to identify their members' strengths to make the group more cohesive.

In addition, I recommend taking personality tests like the Enneagram [10] and the Colors [20] profiling. These are helpful in creating synergy amongst a tribe.

Tribes come together for a shared purpose, something that the tribe can co-create together whether that is a project or a common shared intention. In our case, women are gathering to empower one another in all areas of their lives. The intention is to strengthen our self-love and our relationships with one another. When everyone has a stake in the game – we all see why we are here and the purpose of our gathering – we have the intrinsic motivation to show up and contribute.

Two main intentions form to sustain the tribe: 1) that each individual is seen, heard and valued and 2) that the container of the tribe is honored as sacred so that it doesn't break.

Each individual is working on how she shows up in the tribe, working on the 4 Rs (self-responsibility, self-reliance, self-respect and self-reflection) and her individual intentions. She is working with the tribe as a mirror for her own areas of growth. She is conscious of how her energy affects the whole and mindful of how she impacts the other women in the tribe. She is essentially working on self-acceptance and acceptance of the other women.

The tribe as a whole is then looking at its impact on the outside community and world at large. It treats itself as a collective acting as one entity that exists in the world. So the tribe has a group task, like a project, of how it brings contribution to others. This can be hosting events for the public to experience the tribe's gifts, offering a product or service like selling jewelry and clothing that the tribe designs, or promoting a message and lifestyle that others can emulate.

Each woman must own her own co-creative power with the divine and co-creative power with the other women in the tribe, asking the overarching question of: *How can I serve?*

Tribes fall apart when women ask, *what am I going to get?* This energy comes from the *not good enough* epidemic because we are searching outside of ourselves from what we are really looking to give ourselves: self-love. When we are searching for an answer out there, looking for the tribe to give us something, we are really robbing ourselves from the opportunity to find the answer within. We are essentially looking for unconditional love that we didn't feel we received as a small child. Until we see this, and start to give ourselves the love that we are hungry for, we will always be unsatisfied. The tribe will never be enough.

To get to this place of *how can I serve*, the foundation of the tribe must be based on the importance of self-love, self-acceptance and self-care. Essentially: self-reliance. We do not try to fix, change or heal one another. We hold space for self-healing. We support her in finding the answers within. We listen. We honor her where she is at in her journey, not forcing her to hurry up and get to the point we think she should be at. We trust the process and God's plan for each of us.

The container of a tribe is everything. Holding space for each woman to grow and expand her capacity to love herself and in turn, love others. Holding space for one another to see that we are all worthy exactly as we are, there is nothing for us to do, nowhere for us to go. Just be.

Sometimes, we have to start from this place of *how can I serve* before we get to the place of self-love. Through service, we find ourselves ... our inner strength, our confidence, our self-worth. Through service, we receive a mirror of our greatness. Our sisters tell us how amazing we are. Our sisters acknowledge how we affected them. Our self-love grows with service.

The Tribe Council

To sustain a tribe, each woman must be self-responsible and share responsibility within the tribe. We are all equal partners and owners. This is our tribe. This is my tribe. I am the tribe. You are the tribe. We are one.

Using the vision of twelve women sitting in circle making government decisions together, we create a tribe council for the tribe. Each council member holds her position for a term and has a specific accountability based on her strengths. In addition, a woman can mentor another woman in the tribe who takes on a new accountability.

The tribe council makes sure the container is solid, talking about the needs of the tribe as a whole. The tribe council brings important decisions to the tribe for discussion.

Here's the reality: no one wants to do this part. Everyone wants to show up for themselves when they want. Women are coming to these circles for self-healing, not at a place to serve because their cups are empty. They come to the tribe to fill up. No one wants to do the "work" on the container. Everyone wants the freedom to just be in the container. This is a safe space to go for authentic connection.

What I've witnessed is the growth of women's circles on the phone or in person because there is a huge need right now for this type of work. And yet the model is based on one person's capacity to hold the space.

We must be willing to be trained in developing our leadership. We must be willing to step up so that the current leaders do not get burned out. We must do this work in collaboration, creating a new paradigm of shared responsibility and accountability ... a true circle instead of a hierarchy.

As women, we wait for someone else to take the lead. It is natural as a woman to allow the man to take the lead ... we've been doing it for centuries. Men willingly take action because it is part of their DNA. Our natural way of being is to receive – to allow. To be the flower that opens her petals and waits for the bee to come.

In theory, the Tribe Council sounds brilliant. The vision of a circle of elder women making government decisions sounds powerful and paradigm shifting.

In reality, we have less than 25% of the senate seats occupied by women. Only 18 women were the CEOs of Fortune 500 companies in 2012.

We can point the finger and blame the patriarchy. Or we can look at what's really going on and ask: how do we honor and lead from the feminine? Our natural rhythm? Our natural strengths? And how do we integrate and draw on our inner masculine?

Let's go back to the High Priestess. The woman who is integrated in both her feminine – listening and receiving guidance from spirit – and her masculine – taking action and holding space for others.

What if the Tribe Council, then, was not about doing anything, but instead learning how to be, receive guidance, and powerfully hold space for the intention of the circle? What if the Tribe Council was based completely in the feminine? What if each accountability was not about doing work, but instead holding distinct intentions for the circle based on each Council member's gifts and strengths?

The Tribe Council, then, operates as the container. It can be four women holding the space as the four directions as demonstrated at the Honoring the Masculine-Feminine events. The Tribe Council makes requests to the women in the circle, based on what they see is needed for the forward movement of the circle.

What needs to happen at a gathering? Facilitation. Set up. Clean up. Follow up support structure for the women.

It can be that simple. Tribe Council can hold space, rotate facilitation, and make requests for clean up.

If the tribe wants to expand out and contribute to the outside community or the world at large, the tribe council needs to delegate the specific action steps required to "move" outward.

But if we are operating in the feminine, the rule still applies that all we really need to do is *bloom*, spreading open our petals and allowing others to smell our essence, see our beauty and come closer to have a sniff of what we offer.

In the feminine, there really is nothing much to do. Simply *be* our brilliant, radiant, worthy selves.

The greatest gift we, as a tribe can give, is being the invitation for this lifestyle. Being open for other women to join hands with us and deepen into authentic sisterhood, inspire and empower our men, and unconditionally love our children.

Build the container, be the invitation, and they will come.

Sister Spotlight: Rae's Story

Here I am, bringing women and men together during The Goddess Fest, a magical weekend campout where we celebrate our unique divinity, holistic health, sustainability and the earth. Here I am, joining women from different walks of life, ages, cultures, and countries in an online Global Goddess Glow Sisterhood. Here I am, touring across the country with my band The Moves Collective, sharing my passions of music, connection, the arts while spreading a message of living in the moment. Here I am, being authentically me. Finally.

Now, this wasn't always the case, in fact it was quite the opposite. I grew up with a grounded, loving and supportive family, a good education, enough money, nice friends, and talented in the arts. But I didn't want to be the average "Rachel" that I thought everyone else saw, so I rebelled. While I knew I had an important reason to be here, my self-confidence waned. I went to a ballet school and found myself on the bathroom floor at least daily throwing up what I had eaten that day to try to have the perfect "ballet body" for all of my teen years. I decided to "run away" by leaving high school and home-schooling myself, covering it up with the fact that I was "so determined to be the best dancer I could be". Sure I had drive and passion, but it was built upon a frame that was destined to crash down. I left my home and family as quickly as I left high school and I moved as far away as I could to attend The Boston Conservatory - the top contemporary dance performance college in the US. There I began exploring drugs and alcohol, which quickly became my defense mechanism; I now had a way to numb from those around me and from all the negative dialogue between myself and my body.

As my past relationships began to disintegrate, I began competing with myself and every female whom I crossed paths with, isolating myself to the few guy friends who stuck around for my madness. I pushed and pushed to be this "amazing and beautiful" dancer as it was all that I had until I found myself with 2 fractured shins and a pulled ligament in my spine that disabled me all within three months before graduation! All the lifetime of hard work went down the drain.

I grew during this break from dance and began to feel who I was without my passion and purpose to dance. I was terrified and hated who I was, but as time went on I fell in love with music - something to take away the pain and devastation of my dream as a top performer coming to an end (so I though). I decided that being a starving musician was my only chance towards happiness so I bought a van with all my money, packed it up, and began traveling around the states playing music on the streets for pennies. One day at a time, playing music and leaving my soul on every street corner just to make enough money for my next meal.

With the help of my boyfriend at the time we ended up receiving a lot of support and soon enough we were based in San Diego with our new band, The Moves Collective. Again on the rise I went. We received awards and high appraise for our unique music, but still there were some missing pieces. After a few years of gigging, drinking, partying, flying with the wind, I receive one of the biggest lessons of my life. After a late night gig at a brewery, I got mad at my girlfriend at the time and decided I didn't want to go home with her. In my frustration, tears, and late night delirium I got into my car and sped away. Within minutes I was rolling off the freeway, down a canyon, with no sense of what was actually happening. "A miracle", the cops told me. "Angels were watching", the towing guy told me. "You're meant to be here", my parents and family cried to me. "Don't you see the Rae who we all see, powerful, bold, talented with a heart of gold?" I honestly didn't see any of that at all. Until this moment.

I finally woke up. I am important. I have a reason. My life is precious. No more "you are not enough". I had survived an accident that should have taken my life without one scratch or bruise. Car was totalled, but

I was alive, fresh, and awake to the endless possibilities. I am someone who can make a difference, just by loving each moment of my life and myself endlessly. We are given exactly the situations we need to become the highest version of ourselves. Every day, I pray and thank Great Spirit for that accident ... what a blessing it was!

You may be thinking I'm crazy to say that, but I honestly don't know if I'd be who I am today without that accident. Some people read stories about heroes and heroines and decide that they too want to make a difference. While I had this idea in my head, I never really believed that *I* could be someone to make an impact in the world.

What I've realized is that I don't have to be the ONE to make the difference, all I have to do is make a difference in my own life and inspire others around me to be the best they they can be, love unconditionally, and share happiness. I decided to begin a ripple of peace and harmony in a completely new way.

So the question is presented - how do we sustain the movement?

I believe the most important way we can sustain the movement is to be authentically ourselves. As we each hold a clear vision of what brings us happiness -- what makes our heart thump -- then we can inspire others to do the same. And that will look different for each of us.

Through my experience with Sistership Circle, I have discovered how to listen to my heart authentically. I have learned how to hold space for women to be raw, showing up as they are and feeling supported and accepted in the group. The wisdom and tools that Sistership Circle provides has showed me how to experience internal peace and sister support, giving me the resources to feel confident in starting my own circles and business. I am now LOVING where I'm at on my journey and I support women to do the same in my Goddess Glow Online Sisterhood Circles. I've found beauty through this process of receiving support and allowing the divine feminine energy to flow through me.

Tribe is so important; I believe we all need to feel a sense of belonging so we can do our work on this planet. First by finding peace within ourselves, then understanding our desires and purpose, and finally receiving support from family, the sisterhood, and tribe. From there we sustain the movement as we do what brings us happiness and continue to inspire others to do the same.

~ Rae Ireland

Inquiry Journaling/Affirming Rituals

1. Journal about
   - stepping into your leadership as a high priestess
   - letting go, accepting and forgiving
   - sustaining your personal energy through self-care
   - expressing your essence through your sexuality
   - owning your worth and living prosperously.

2. Journal about any "cracks" in your foundation as a woman and how you will go about mending them.

Part 3: Holding a Feminine Container for the World

I am a New Generation Feminine Leader
I am a new generation feminine leader.
And I never lead alone.
I want to do this together
Because I know the power of two over one.

I have surrendered into the feminine
There is nothing to prove.
I have no desire for positions or titles
Just a need to move

Forward not backwards
Let's stop repeating past fears
Hatred and discrimination
Are our ego's reflections and mirrors.

The world needs us sisters to co-create
A new model of love and peace
Generations coming together
Grandmother, aunt, sister and niece.

I lead from my heart.
I lead because I must.
I lead from my soul.
The world needs more of us.

Leadership is not about separation
Of us versus them.

It's about unity and connectedness
Knowing that you are my friend.

Now it's time, women, to lay down our swords
We're not here to conquer and win
Let's open our hearts and arms
To embrace and welcome our men.

Everyone belongs in this circle.
Forgiveness and acceptance are a must.
Leave no one behind
The world includes all of us.

Chapter 12: How We Hold Our Men

"I inspire and empower the masculine to provide and protect."

The men just wouldn't let up. No matter how much I resisted, they kept asking to be part of Tribal Truth.

Barry started it. At our LA Launch in Feb 2011, Barry showed up to take photos. No one that I knew of asked him to. He was just ... there. He fit right in though and when we chatted afterwards, he said he was available to help when we wanted to start the men's division, whatever that looked like.

I thought about it. Tribal Truth for men. I had many conversations with my romantic partner at the time about being the man to start it. When he voiced his need for a men's group, I immediately launched into how it could be Tribal Truth and the benefits of putting it under our brand name. He wasn't interested. He didn't want to partner. So his men's group went on for nine months while I kept my mouth shut.

In a way, my vision died. I let it go. I closed the door. I focused on empowering women to step into their leadership to save the world because the men weren't worth anything. They didn't listen. They weren't showing up. They were doing their own thing.

Co-Creative Leadership at that time wasn't about co-creating as humanity. I was missing half of the planet. I was only focused on women co-creating with one another.

It didn't even occur to me that I was so angry and spiteful toward men that I would completely exclude them from my efforts to "save the world." How ignorant I was, completely unconscious about my relationship with the masculine.

However, with my interest in traditional tribe roots and culture, there was no way I could prevent the natural integration of men into the tribe. In September 2012, I went to a Native American ceremony called Long Dance. [21] One hundred twenty-five women danced around a fire and performed rituals for healing from sunset to sunrise. Eighteen men guarded the perimeter of the sacred site so that the women could do their deep work. The site was surrounded by hills. A drumbeat started the ceremony at sunset and continued without pause until sunrise.

As the sun peaked over the ridge top to the east, the drumbeat stopped. Everyone stopped and turned to face the sun. Shadow outlines of the men started to appear. The leader blew a conch shell and the men began to chant a Native American morning song to the women.

My heart expanded and I choked up with emotion. What touched me was the act of selfless service these men provided us so we could do our deep work. It took courage and strength to dance around the fire the entire night. Many women experienced profound healing and let go of past traumas during the ceremonies. We felt safe, we felt supported, and we felt protected by the men.

I imagined for a moment what the world would look like if men and women gave this kind of love and support for one another. If we honored one another's process. If we unconditionally loved one another in a way that held space for the other.

At that moment, I realized that Tribal Truth could no longer exist as a "women only" organization. We cannot do it alone. We need to include our men. We need to embrace the masculine as our partner, not an enemy. The world does not work with an imbalance of masculine and feminine energy.

As I shared this story with the conscious men in my life, I learned how much men wanted to be part of the work we have been doing. Many men shed tears, moved by the feminine honoring of the masculine. Every man said YES, I'm in.

One man in particular stepped up and said he would start the Tribal Truth Divine Brotherhood. He became the catalyst for this vision to become a reality. He saw an opportunity to create a safe space for men to empower one another and show up for women as embodied warriors. This man played an interesting role in the creation of this new vision. He came in like a spark plug and combusted, leaving just as quickly as he entered the scene.

During that first month of January 2013, I was stuck thinking: *"I don't know how to do this. I don't know how to empower the men. I don't know how to bring them into the circle. This one isn't the one. It's not a man who is supposed to start this."*

On a walk through the lagoon near my house one day, it came to me. Tribe. The four directions. Four women. No, it's not the men to start it. It's me. It's through co-creation. It's women holding space for men.

⁂

Three women's names came to me at that moment and I hurried home to call them in my inspired state. I shared my vision of creating a feminine container that empowers and inspires the masculine to take action.

A few days later, the four of us came together to co-create the first event to bring in the men. I knew all three but they didn't know each other, so each woman introduced herself and why she felt called to co-create this event. We all came to the same conclusion: We will not assume. We will ask questions. We will listen. We will honor what the masculine has to say.

And so, the first *Honoring the Masculine* occurred on Sunday Feb 24, 2013. Men came to be heard. Came to be honored. Came to share their voice. Came for brotherhood. Came for union with the feminine. Women came to listen. Came to hold space. Came to embody unconditional love for our men.

This event was a catalyst for what is possible when we truly seek to understand. Partnership is satisfying the other person's needs. For us to create true balanced partnership on the planet, we, as women, must understand what our men need. This is the first step to create that partnership that will transform the world.

I crashed the next day, overwhelmed by the intensity of holding space for ninety people. Overwhelmed by the emotion. One of the co-facilitators crashed, too. We spoke about riding the high and then not having the support afterwards to hold us.

After an intense event, the feminine must hold and nurture the feminine. I realized then that I needed to make sure my support structure was in place for the day after.

I needed to be held physically.
I needed love.
I needed to be honored.
I needed acknowledgment.
I needed celebration.
I needed rest.
I needed to release anything that I had picked up energetically in the process of holding the container.

While overwhelmed, I also felt extremely powerful. I felt like my glow was ON, my feminine essence radiant.

A week before the event, I drew three goddess cards from my Doreen Virtue deck: "High Priestess," "Leap of Faith" and "True Love."

"You are going to meet your man at *Honoring the Masculine,* " my best friend and roommate, Anat said to me. I brushed it off at the time, but on Tuesday, I was thinking about all the amazing men who showed up on Sunday and wondering whom I would connect with.

On Wednesday, we had an intimacy discussion at my house and when I walked down the stairs, J- was standing at the bottom of the staircase. He was one of the guys from the event who left an impression on me.

I gave him a big hug, excited to see him and talk about the event. I told him my vision of creating *Honoring the Feminine* next.

He stopped me dead in my tracks. "I invite you to allow the men to create that event for you women. Do you think you would be able to let go of control and turn it over?"

Intrigued, I asked him if he would want to step up and do that. "Not me. I am not a leader in the community. In my humility, I would support other men in doing it, but I'm not in a place to lead."

I wanted to continue the conversation, but got pulled away. When the discussion started, I immediately zeroed in on J- and sat next to him. When I get focused on something I want, I am very intentional. In this case, I wanted to continue to talk with this man who presented a challenge for me.

Letting go of control. Allowing the men to step up, create and serve. Trusting. It pushed every button. It challenged my leadership. Game on.

At the end of the discussion, J- asked me, "Can I have you?"

Startled and confused, I responded: "Excuse me?"

"Can I have your attention?"

I relaxed a little, guard still up slightly. "Sure."

Everyone moved out of the living room and we were alone.

"First, I want to create a boundary. I will not kiss you and I ask that you don't kiss me. I don't want there to be any sexual energy so we can connect intimately without that worry."

I immediately relaxed, respecting this man for such a direct request. "And I am attracted to you, just so you know. I think you are beautiful."

I smiled. I felt the attraction too. We talked for two hours. At the end, I invited him to my birthday party the next evening. He wanted to date. I liked him. I felt safe.

J- and I had a good run for three months — diving head first into a romantic and business partnership — and then lost steam and went our separate ways. It was as if we were destined to meet, twin flames sparking something within each other. J- embodied the masculinity in all its glory. I learned a very important lesson about the High Priestess and a new model of partnership and co-creative leadership ... it goes back to a critical sentence I said earlier that I will repeat again here:

Tribe. The four directions. Four women. No, it's not the men to start it. It's me. It's through co-creation. It's the women holding space for the men ... creating a feminine container that empowers and inspires the masculine to take action.

Women, it's time to step into a new relationship with ourselves, with each other and with the men on this planet.

- I must embody the High Priestess, independent, fierce, **cleansed**, free, and able to hold space.
- I must partner with my sisters to create a feminine container for the world.
- We, the sisterhood, must hold that container to inspire and empower our men to take the action and do the work.
- We simply hold space. We simply BE the change. We simply glow and radiate with our feminine essence to INSPIRE.

Simple, but not easy. I kept forcing a man to step up. I kept looking for a man to lead. I kept waiting. I kept hitting my head on the wall over and over again as it didn't work out.

My dream shattered with the breakup with J-. But instead of closing my heart from hurt and pain, I opened it wider. No more co-dependency. No more looking out there for change.

The High Priestess looks within. She is solid in her knowing, deep in her trust, connected. The High Priestess is the female leader of a tribe, religion, or movement; a female high priest. She performs spiritual rituals. When I stepped into creating the ritual for the *Honoring the Masculine*, I stepped into the embodiment of High Priestess. To me, it symbolizes a way of being where I am my best self, fully in my power.

Integrated in my masculine and feminine.
Grounded in reality and spiritually connected.
Tapped into my intuition.
Glowing in my radiance.
Magnetic and attractive because I am a clear channel.
Expansive and full of love and light.
Powerful in my knowing and trust in my leadership.
Owning my value and worth.
Sensual, creative and soft.
Direct, clear on my boundaries, unshakeable.
Vulnerable, sweet and compassionate.

This is the feminine container. It's embodied. It inspires. It empowers. Accepting, loving, compassionate, powerful. People listen. A pin drop can be heard in the space. Rapt attention. A quickening of the heart and a silencing of the mind.

It is when I embody the High Priestess that I call in the masculine to show up to serve (provide and protect) because I am open and present to receiving. This is the dance, and yet it is so confronting. To call upon our higher self as women takes strength, determination and humility.

It requires us to fill our cup and be in a place of generosity and service without needing anything in return. It requires us to be in tune with our body and integrate our mind and heart. It requires us to be in full surrender and trust of the divine, which lies within our own self. It requires us to love unconditionally, starting with the self.

It requires us to remember who we are as divine beings of light and love. I've done the work and yet the work is not done. The journey is a lifelong process.

The High Priestess is a way of being we must choose over and over again despite the challenges of everyday life — mindful in the ebb and flow, conscious with the mundane, aware of the circumstances. And the process is one of the continual opening of our hearts.

What J- and I created together in a month is far beyond what I had created in three years. The three years working with the women in Tribal Truth brought me to this place of being able to easily create so much with J- in a month; it laid a foundation and prepared me to step into High Priestess in my life and my business.

Being the High Priestess is a context for how I show up in the world. For this I am eternally grateful for this angel of a man coming into my life to open my heart.

Sister Spotlight: Peta's Story

To hold a man is sacred. It takes deep awareness of the self and of your relationship with the masculine. In order to hold our men, we must inspire them by fully owning our feminine divinity. Becoming a Sistership Circle Facilitator taught me how to be a woman who inspires, a woman who knows herself, a woman who accepts all that she is and loves herself for it, a woman who can lead with beauty, grace and wisdom ... a woman who can Hold Our Men.

My relationship with the masculine has taken many forms: love, hate, fear, judgement, joy, safety, resentment, understanding, compassion and respect. I feel blessed for the many lessons I have learned along the way and for those I continue to learn as I raise my 3 boys together with my husband.

When I was a child I remember always being amongst boys. I have an older brother and most of my cousins are boys. So as the youngest girl trying to fit in with the boys, I always felt a bit isolated as I would be the easy target to tease; I developed a sense of 'less than'. However I also found strength because anything they did I was determined to do as well. So I had a motorbike and a windsurfer, and I went fishing and camping but somehow I knew I still didn't quite fit in. I never wanted to be a boy, I loved be girly. Yes I rode motorbikes but of course I did it with pink gloves!!

When I started dating, I was looking for Mr Prince Charming. He would be strong, handsome and take care of me. We would fall in love, get married, have babies and live happily ever after. The man I attracted was far from that. The first man that I slept with, that I loved, was an abusive narcissist. For five years I was manipulated, humiliated and degraded. I tried so hard to fix him with my love, clinging to this notion that if only I did it better everything would be alright. I had no self-esteem and I was frightened; I felt so powerless. I was a victim of abuse. This was such a shock to me, how could I have become this woman? I finally left him; I literally had to escape and move interstate because he threatened to kill me.

I was so angry towards men; they were pathetic so I used and abused them because I thought this is what being a powerful woman looked like. Use your beauty to seduce them and buy you things, then leave them for the next one. But I was wrong; I actually kept abusing myself because all along I really wanted one of them to love and save me.

I found out I was 22 weeks pregnant when I was travelling in the UK, I was 25 and just about to head off on an African Safari. Instead I flew home to Australia to birth my beautiful first son. My parents were so supportive and I was love-struck with this little being, my son, how precious. I felt so in love and in awe of myself for creating such a perfect baby – I am woman hear me roar! Yes I was a single mother and yes I felt alone and scared at times and sadly I felt shame for getting "knocked up" overseas. I remember one of my dad's friends saying to me whilst I was heavily pregnant "You're going to find it very difficult to get a man now you know, no one's going to want to take on a single mum."

I know now that this is *his* story, not mine.

It took me another 2 years to figure out that if I didn't show myself love and respect then how could I expect a man to do the same towards me? So I made a pledge to accept nothing less than the best, because that's what I deserved. I wrote a list of attributes that I wanted in a man. On our wedding day I read out that list to our guests – I had summoned him, I had called to him and he showed up.

In Sistership Circle we have the ability to learn about ourselves so deeply. We are given the tools to really uncover our shit and see it all. Only when we allow ourselves to shine a light on it can we be free. I have been working with Reiki energy for over 15 years and I have been meditating and communing with Angels and other divine beings for over 20 years. As I combined my knowledge of these things with the teachings and tools from Sistership Circle, I grew more rapidly than any other time in my life. I was ready. The Universe, Great Spirit, Grand Mysterio had led me on the perfect path to empowerment, Divine Feminine Empowerment. I humbly continue to grow each day.

One of the lessons I learned from Circle was to understand that our lives are a mirror; we are provided with a reflection of all that we need to know and learn so that we can become more empowered. We create similar situations so that we can get **it**; only when we really see **it** and understand **it** can we move on. And then the universe will pop a reminder in every now and then so that we can see **it** more quickly and use the tools we've learned to navigate through.

Now, my husband is not abusive nor is he narcissistic in any way; he is very honourable. Yet his story and his experiences have taught him that he must provide, protect (very typical masculine qualities that I respect) but he also needs to fix and save. I don't want to be saved. I have all the power I need within myself, so how am I still creating this role of victim? Where am I not seeing this in my own story?

I had to dig deep for this one.

Between the age of 5 and 7 my father's best friend sexually abused me *every other Friday night.*

I wanted someone to save me from that so badly, but I became silent. I tried to give clues but no one heard me. So eventually I confided in my mum and we never saw him again. It was such a huge relief to finally say something, be heard and believed, but it was such a massive thing to process so I diminished it, blew it off as "not that big a deal."

But it continued to show up.

Through self-reflection and discovery, I realised that I had lost my innocence back then, a man had taken away my power at such a young age and I was crying out to be saved again and again during my life. This experience had created the story of men being something to fear and that I needed to be saved.

What I also discovered was that I had actually saved myself as that young girl of 7 – I used my voice, I spoke up.

I believe violence is born from fear, hurt and abuse.

Domestic Violence is at epidemic proportions:

2 women are killed each week on average in Australia.

1 woman is hospitalised every 3 hours.

Children see and hear the violence too.

How can we as a society put an end to this level of violence?

Personally, as a feminine leader, I feel it is my responsibility to embody the feminine essence within me that is the creator, the inspiration, the glue, the binding force that provides and holds the container full of love for my men so that they may thrive and make the world a better place.

Collectively, as a Sisterhood we have a responsibility to hold our men in such a way that they honour and respect not only themselves but others, in particular women, the feminine.

~ Peta Bastian

Inquiry Journaling/Affirming Rituals

1. How often do you allow men to contribute and serve the feminine?

2. How often do you reject a man's desire to help and contribute to you (including little things like carrying your heavy bag)?

3. What is your relationship with setting and holding clear boundaries?

Chapter 13: Honoring the Masculine

"I partner with men."

It's our responsibility. It's our responsibility to hold our men and stop blaming and shaming them. It's our responsibility to embody unconditional love and hold them like a baby in a blanket. It's our responsibility to listen, let go of judgment, listen, let go of being right, listen, and keep listening. It's our responsibility to be the light. It's our responsibility to take a stand for peace and harmony. It's our responsibility.

They are confused. They are wounded. They are ashamed. This is not said to diminish men, but to evoke compassion, understanding and empathy. Whatever he did to you, he was doing the best he could with the limited knowledge he had.

But ...

No buts. You think your story is unique and special. You think you had it the worst. You are fuming, ready to shut this book because you are right Goddammit, he did it to you and you cannot forgive him, but you must.

You must.
We must.
Forgive.

If we continue to hold grudges, seek revenge, blame, shame, guilt, punish, admonish, and argue, we will never win. The world will never change. Israel and Palestine will continue to fight for eternity until one side lets go of being right. Is this what we want?

Is being *right* more important than *peace*? Is getting *revenge and winning* more important than *love*? We have to let go. We have to forgive. Surrender is not a weakness; it is the feminine's greatest strength.

To love and forgive someone despite the evil and destructive harm they have caused you is far more powerful than blaming and continuing the pattern of hate.

The masculine is not bad, wrong, evil or even vicious. The masculine has been wounded. Like a wounded deer trying to survive against the wolves, it fights back with fear and scarcity.

The masculine on our planet has been operating from a wounded place, disconnected from the feminine, hurting the feminine, creating an imbalance, disharmony, and disease.

The feminine does not by its nature fight back, force its way back, and try to tip the scales back in her favor. She loves. She forgives. She allows. She receives. Light fills the dark. Love overpowers the fear.

⁂

The feminine knows who she is. She knows her power. She knows her worth. She knows she is the ultimate co-creator. She knows. The feminine honors, loves, accepts, and cares for herself. So when she meets the masculine, she is filled up, an overflowing cup of abundant love and joy.

She is connection. She is affinity. This is her essence. When she is in her power — the high priestess, goddess, queen, mother, lover — she inspires. She stops the masculine dead in his tracks. He completely forgets what he was doing and is entranced by her beauty. She is breathtaking. It is in that moment, the pause between breaths when the world stops, that anything is possible.

I have heard that the feminine is the Holy Grail. She is the thing to get to. She is the centerpiece. She is the inspiration.

You, as a woman, have both feminine and masculine energy/ qualities/attributes. You, as a woman, the embodiment of love, must learn how to accept and nurture yourself first to bring light into the world. This is how you meet the men of this world: as whole, embodied, full, radiant, loving, accepting, nurturing, listening, honoring.

Honoring the masculine within myself. Honoring the masculine within him. Allowing him. Receiving him. Loving him. Forgiving him.

He just wants to contribute. Allow him. Tell him how he can show up for you. It does not make you weak. Receiving is your strength. Allowing is your power.

He just wants to provide. Allow him. Tell him what you need and desire. Tell him what would make you happy. Happiness is your beauty. Joy is your freedom.

He just wants to feel like he belongs, like you do. He just wants to feel worthy, like you do. He just wants to be accepted, like you do. Men are designed to be physically bigger, stronger, and faster than us so they can build for us, protect us, and feed us.

Imagine being a man today … food is already provided. Homes are already built. Women already have jobs and their own money. And you are rejected, blamed and shamed by the women of the world.

Seek to understand. Empathize with their role in the world today. We have been leaving them behind as we connect together in sisterhood tribes to change the world. It's time to reach out our arms and invite them into the feminine container we are creating.

Partnership

It's simple to say forgive men, forgive the masculine, and yet it is not easy. When the next boyfriend after J- broke up with me (on my Maui vacation with my entire family), I shut down. I fumed. I raged.

I felt betrayed. Abandoned. Hurt. Thrown out. I felt unappreciated, unseen, and undervalued. How could he not see who I had been for him? How could he walk away from the relationship so coldly and closed off? After all we shared, he had no gratitude in his heart. He couldn't see me clearly for who I really was. I knew I had to let go, forgive and move on.

So the first thing I did was completely cut him off. This was the hardest thing in the world, because all I wanted to do was call him and cry and beg him to come back and admit he made a mistake. But he didn't make a mistake. This breakup was happening for a reason.

I cut him off so I could really get the message. I couldn't see clearly if I was engaging with him because then I would get caught in the story of it all and not the truth.

The truth was there was a pattern. My pattern. I slowly started to see it. I got curious. The only way I could truly create the partnership I was looking for with a man was by tracing this pattern all the way back in time and pulling it out by the root. I needed to completely release this anger, indignation, and frustration toward the masculine. I needed to completely feel the grief underneath it all and integrate that little girl who was crying out for unconditional love.

It always goes back to our fathers.

Oh Daddy I love you so much. Oh Daddy I want you to take care of me. Oh Daddy please be my hero.

A memory hit me a couple weeks after the breakup: that scene where I was arguing with my brother in the backseat of the car. Dad reaching back to slap me.

Shut up.
Shut down.
What you have to say doesn't matter.
I'm in charge.
Do as I say.
If you talk back, you will suffer the consequences.

I was the scapegoat. The big sister who should know better than to torment her little brother.

Stop trying to get the last word.
Knock it off, Tanya.
Give it a rest.
You'll never win.

I was feeling that same anger, indignation, frustration. It wasn't fair. Always a struggle. Trapped. Can't get out of the car. Sit in your shit and fume. Swallow it. Stop talking. What you have to say doesn't matter. You can never change his mind. You are invisible.

Invisible.
Invisible.
Invisible.

Small. Insignificant. Second tier.

Daddy, comfort me. Daddy, tell me I'm ok. Tell me it's going to be all right. Tell me how much you love me.

As I write this, tears are streaming down my face. I can feel my little girl crying out for his attention. I can feel her hurting so much. I forgive you, Daddy, for you didn't know any better. You didn't know.

My dad was my hero. He provided everything I could have ever asked for. The toys, the house, the vacations. Indian Princesses. Camping. Adventures just me and him. He coached my softball team. He and my best friend's dad were the best coaches ever and everyone loved them. He was kind and an excellent teacher. He cared so much about us.

I remember him piling eight of us little girls in his 911 Porsche. I had to sit in the middle and he taught me how to shift the gears as he guided my hand with his. I thought he was so cool.

I remember him coming into my room. I was brushing my teeth in my bathroom. He started crying. I must have been around twelve years old. Upset about business. The economy. Why he was crying to me, I don't know. Apologizing for not being able to be the man he wanted to be for me?

He loved us so much. He worked so hard. He provided, and yet he didn't protect me from my brother. I've gone from boy to boy, man to man, searching for my daddy, searching for that unconditional love. Searching to be saved.

I know he didn't mean it. I know he didn't have any clue as to the impact on me. My adult rational mind knows that this is just what he learned from his parents and he was reacting to his own anger and frustration.

And yet my little girl felt so lost. So confused. So unloved, unseen, unheard. And so fucking angry. How could he? How could he? How could he?

So I associated money with support. That was the way he provided his love. That's what I could count on. "I can't meet your emotional needs, Tanya. I can't provide you what you need, but I can provide you everything else."

This is a common inconsistency and confusion of the masculine in my life. They simply don't know how to provide that comfort I crave so badly, that unconditional love.

I can see it play out over and over again. Asking my best guy friend to "protect" me from another little boy in eighth grade ... pushed him off his bike to beat him up. Being shot by another guy friend while I was with another guy. He got jealous and shot me in the leg. I still have the pellet in my calf.

Wounded boy after wounded boy ... suicide attempts, drug use, pathological lying. Physically pushed. A pillow over my face.

And that indignation. Rage when I felt like I wasn't been heard. Fuming when I felt invisible and unappreciated. I can forgive because I know who my dad was for me. I can forgive because I know he loved me so much.

And I feel.

I feel the grief of my little girl self so hurt and upset and confused. I cry her tears. I hold her and comfort her because she felt all alone and misunderstood. I stroke her hair and tell her she is seen and loved. I tell her she's safe. Safe.

We close our hearts to the masculine because we don't feel safe. We shut down and stay silent because it has been dangerous in the past to speak our truth.

A slap. A beating. Punishment. A conviction. Guilty. In trouble. And all alone.

When my boyfriend broke up with me in Maui, I should have told him to go home. Instead, I suffered in silence, just as I did in that car ride as a child because I was told to keep my mouth shut. I accommodated him. I didn't want to jeopardize anything. I was guilty as charged and had to take responsibility for my actions.

I've seen countless other women in situations with men where they suffered in silence. Kept her mouth shut while having sex. Kept her mouth shut while allowing his hand to move up her breast.

We can rationalize it all we want, but the truth is this pattern keeps repeating over and over again until we fully allow ourselves to go back in time to the thing we are trying to get.

We are all trying to get something from the masculine. We are trying to get unconditional love. We are searching for the thing we, as little girls, had missed. We are replaying the tragedy over and over again, playing the victim, the martyr and even the perpetrator. The cycle will continue until we bring awareness to the truth, feel the grief, and then fully let it go.

We must release our father from being our prisoner. Let him go. Stop holding him hostage. Release him and all the others. They have suffered enough. *I release you, Daddy. I love you for who you are and who you are not. I forgive you.*

⁂

The partnership we are looking for as women is created when we stop trying to get something from them. This "taking" energy comes through wanting money, security, comfort, emotional support, protection and love.

Men feel suffocated and don't want to give us anything when we demand it, act entitled to it, and want to take it from them. They feel drained, used and inadequate.

I didn't fully get this until my last two boyfriends told me exactly that. I didn't see it until I finally sat down with myself to receive the message and that memory of my dad came up.

I am so drained by it that all I want to do is go to sleep. I want to numb out. I have been holding on so tightly and don't want to let go and in turn, it has been holding onto me so tightly that I have been exhausted chasing and trying to get something from the masculine.

The answer lies in unconditionally loving them. The partnership we so deeply desire happens when we unconditionally love them no matter what. I have so many wonderful memories of my dad. I can list hundreds of reasons to love him. I am very clear on who he has been for me and how big he showed up in my world. I am present to his brilliance, his sacrifice and his love.

His kindness.
His gentleness.
His desire to do good.
His generosity.
His commitment to my family.
His partnership with my mom for over 40 years.
His intelligence.
His fun and adventurous spirit.

And on and on ...

My adult mind knows all of this and so does yours. And it has kept me from paying attention to a part of myself that was still wounded and silently suffering. Because what the mind is attached to blocks the emotion from being integrated.

And I kept feeling that indignation in my relationships, justifying and rationalizing it, instead of getting to the source of it and feeling the hurt little girl acting out enraged, trying to get someone to comfort her and love her unconditionally.

When that little girl feels safe enough to cry in front of her daddy, let it all out, wail and sob uncontrollably because she knows he's got her and will love and support her unconditionally, she can then let it all go and be free of the misery.

From that freedom, she softens. From the softness, she opens. From the opening, she inspires. She inspires and he shows up to serve. When we step into real forgiveness, we can be the catalyst for true partnership.

True Partnership occurs when both people ...

Enter the relationship whole
Take personal responsibility
Want to give unconditionally
Practice awareness of the impact of any and all actions on the other person

Ask the other person what (s)he needs
Create a context that is bigger than the two individuals
Want to create win-win-win
Don't care about being right
Care about love and affinity being present at all times
Lean in
Create space and freedom
Commit to the partnership
Love unconditionally

When you catch yourself complaining about the masculine – how he isn't showing up, not taking the lead, or shutting down – this is an indication for you to do your own work. This is your cue to tap into the feeling arising in your body and trace it back in time. Allow the feeling to carry you back instead of searching for it.

These feelings will arise in your partnerships. Relationships are mirrors of ourselves and so they bring us everything we need to heal. You are in the right place. You are exactly where you need to be. Keep doing your work.

Sister Spotlight: Elena's Story

The work that I have done in Circle has helped me become more connected to myself. And the more connected I am to myself, the more connected I am to my husband and my son. It is nice to feel my soul and not just live from the neck up. I've been so inspired by this work that I have become a circle facilitator and really enjoy watching the transformation that Sistership Circle has in women. I love hearing from women who wished I went to visit their town so that they too could benefit from a circle.

CHAPTER 13: HONORING THE MASCULINE

Before Circle, I was so busy doing things and getting everything right that my life was nothing more than a blur. It was through the amazing connection to myself that I developed in Circle that I realized that my family was not just 3 people who lived at the same address.

One day it hit me, "they love me!" They really do; my husband and my son adore me. I mean the world to them as much as they mean the world to me. They appreciate me, and they are here in *our* home living *with me*. This realization got me to appreciate their love and absorb it in a way that I hadn't done before. I could feel my husband's love even if he wasn't saying anything. Obviously he wasn't just randomly living in our home, he chose to be here with me, raising our son and building a family together. How delicious is that?

Acknowledging my commitment and my dedication made me appreciate my husband's commitment and dedication. Even if in my mind I had known this all along, I didn't have a connection to what it really meant. My love for our son has always been strong but my patience has definitely increased. My love connection to him precedes my need to correct his behavior and when I do, it is with more love and respect than ever before.

Now to the juicy part … the circle work resolved some of the sexual issues I had. Before Circle, I had an ongoing struggle feeling like my husband only wanted one thing and lacked the tact to seduce me. I complained that his approach was one of a predator or an abuser.

However, I realized that the reason I felt this way was because I had been abused and I had experienced a predator ex-husband. This changed when I became a master of receiving his masculine energy; I began to accept his approach as his way of showing me his desire.

I realized that if I was in high school, I would've been excited if a boy wanted to get close to me. So if I hadn't had any of the abusive experiences, I'd probably still be excited to have a man approach me, signaling his interest in me.

From that moment on, I decided that my husband deserved a better reaction from me, my "high school" reaction. This approach made me more connected and eager to receive his love and affection.

Lastly, through Circle I learned how to lean in for support from my husband. I have always been all power in my life. There is no obstacle that I can't tackle. No matter what, I didn't need anyone's help. I didn't mean for this survivor approach to apply to men specifically, but it ended up applying to my husband. He'd watch me do everything and never ask for help. My husband actually decided that I had a big ego. However, for me, it wasn't about ego, it was about not knowing when to lean in and ask for support.

It took many years, but I finally did it. I leaned in and asked him to support us financially for a couple of months while I recovered from a health issue. It was hard to ask, but I was determined to be my new self and lean into the discomfort of asking.

What came out of my mouth the first time I asked was accusatory. I had to regroup and ask again. The second time, I stood in my power, made myself vulnerable and I honored his support with my request. His response was a simple "ok." There was no shame, no second-guessing, no upset

Ask and be prepared to receive, what a concept!

Today, I am fully in my relationship and every cell of my body knows what that means, not just my head.

~ Elena MacGregor

Inquiry Journaling/Affirming Rituals

1. Journal about your partnership with men. What unfinished work do you need to do to create full and meaningful relationships with the men in your life?

Chapter 14: This Is for Our Children

"All is well. Everything is as it is supposed to be. Perfect."

They say the people in your life come in for a reason, a season or a lifetime. I want to add: Everyone who comes into our life comes in to teach us something.

We have the most to learn from the people who trigger us the most because they are mirroring a part of ourselves that we haven't integrated and accepted yet. They are a blessing if you open yourself up to receive their contribution, no matter how painful and frustrating.

And then there are the angels. The people who come into your life who deliver something so sweet, so precious that you feel they are a kindred spirit.

One woman came into my life in 2013 as a participant of my *Leading In Truth* retreat, revealing herself as one of my angels.

Karen Solomon came over to my house for lunch a few weeks before the retreat to get to know me and see if the retreat was a good fit for her. Little did I know that she would activate my greatest healing so I could cross the threshold from girl to woman.

I had been exploring "what it means to be a woman" since the first *Honoring the Masculine*, but didn't ever quite feel like I had "grown into" being a woman yet.

Karen shared with me on my couch that her biggest regret was not making the choice to have children. When she married, her husband didn't want children. Not having made a choice either way, she went with his decision.

As she looked me in the eyes, tears welling, she asked me if I wanted children. "If you could get one thing from me, I want you to feel fully empowered to choose and know for yourself yes or no. Not maybe," she said to me.

I felt the yes, but hesitated. I hadn't felt clear. There was so much in the way.

Three years earlier, at the *Celebration of Woman* retreat, I saw how I had judged my own mother for just being a stay-at-home-mom. I didn't want to be anything like that. I didn't want to sacrifice my goals and dreams to be a mother. But at the retreat, I came to accept her choice and see it as a choice. Her purpose was motherhood. It was what she desired. I found respect for her choice, but was left unsure of my own relationship to motherhood.

If I became a mother, did I have to give up everything else? Could I manage it all? Would I be a good mother if I prioritized my work in the world over my family?

Deep down, I wanted to be a mother. I loved children. It was just fear in the way. "Yes," I said.

I realized four months later that everything in my life shifted to support that intention: A man showed up to be my partner in healing that final piece around my father. The healers showed up to guide me to integrate my inner child and clear out all that was in my way. The grief showed up as I let go of my old identity.

I had been running myself into the ground, becoming so resentful and burned out trying to uphold my organization. I had been leading from a place of proving my self-worth because I thought if I wasn't doing all of what I was doing, I had no place in the world and I didn't matter.

It hit me how beautifully perfect 2013 summer's process had been no matter how uncomfortable and difficult. I was letting go of that point of view that I wasn't enough.

And through that process, I started to experience what it felt like to just be and do very little and still make a difference. Because for the first time in my life, I was making a difference for myself.

I embodied self-acceptance.

I learned self-love.

I practiced self-care.

This is what it means to be a woman. We don't need to save the world at the expense of our own freedom. I know now that when I step into what's next and build from this place, I will be in my fullest expression. My children will learn what it looks like for a woman to take care of herself and be of service to the world.

Integrating, Loving and Accepting My Inner Child

The child who you were is still inside of you. That childlike joy, the innocence, the playfulness, the spontaneity, the freedom ... it is all still inside of you.

This integration piece is absolutely critical to the evolution of humanity. We have been shutting down that voice inside of us that is crying for help. We have been stifling, locking her up, closing her off, afraid that we won't be accepted if we act "childish."

We went through childhood and teenage years being told to "grow up" and we wanted to be like the adults. As an adult, we wish we could be a kid again. We don't realize it, but we are looking for our lost innocence.

I've found that the more I integrate the shadow side and feel those suppressed childhood feelings, the more innocent and joyful I become. I feel so young again, but I also feel so much wiser. I feel whole.

This process of getting in touch with little five-year-old Tanya has allowed me to appreciate myself and all that I have been through.

She's the one who has the self-doubt, the fear, the insecurity, the worry. She didn't know any better. She didn't have the tools that I have now.

Dear Tanya,

You are safe. I've got you. You can come curl up in a ball with your blanket next to me. I've got you. I'll stroke your hair and hold you tight. I've got you.

It's okay to cry. It's okay to be scared. The world seems big and overwhelming to you. I've got you.

I see you. You are so ambitious and hard working. You are so smart and athletic. I am impressed with how much you strive to learn. And it's okay if you mess up. I've got you.

I hear you. You so badly want to be heard. You want to know that your voice matters. That what you say is equally important. I've got you.

I love you. I am so glad you were born. You are so special. You can do anything you want in this world. I've got you.

Your little brother also just wants to be seen, heard and loved. I know he's loud and a pain, but he just wants attention. He wants your attention. Can you show him how much you love him no matter how annoying he can be? I've got you.

Your mom loves you so much. She wanted so badly to have a baby and here you are, her little angel. She didn't mean to hurt you by giving your brother attention. He's just smaller than you. She tried to give you both equal love and attention. Can you forgive your little brother for needing your mom's attention? I've got you.

I've got you.
I'm not going anywhere.
I'm holding you.

You can trust me.
I love you.
Love, Tanya

In Kindergarten, my classmate had a seizure on the playground one day. She shook and convulsed on the blacktop. Shocked, I stared. I didn't know what it meant, but it scared me. The ambulance came and took her away.

Later that year, she died. Our class gathered in a circle in the soccer field to say prayers for her passing. No one cried except one boy. He couldn't understand why no one else was crying.

I was embarrassed. She was a strange girl; no one was friends with her. I felt numb. Was I supposed to cry? I didn't miss her. It was sad, but I wasn't sad.

In 2002, I taught English in Japan. One couple, a Japanese woman and an American man, welcomed all of us teachers and took us on trips around the countryside during the two weeks before we started school. They had a four-year-old son who came everywhere with us.

I always worried about that little boy because he didn't have any rules and would run around loose, no one watching him. Something's going to happen to him if his parents aren't careful, I thought.

Then one day, one of the English teachers knocked on my door, crying. "That little boy fell off a bridge and died." Four years old.

I went to the house for the funeral and that same feeling came over me. Numbness. It was sad, but I wasn't sad. I couldn't understand it. I loved that little boy. But I couldn't feel anything.

A few months later, one of my students, a seventh grader was hit by a car and died. Same numbness. Same lack of feeling.

As I lay on the healer's table recounting these memories, the grief for all three children swept over me and I cried. I sobbed. I felt the pain. I felt the sadness.

I immediately knew what had been stopping me from wanting to be a mother. I identified the feeling underneath the fear and by integrating it into my present day body, I now feel free to step into motherhood.

Motherhood to me symbolizes something so much greater than giving birth to a baby. Motherhood to me is the ultimate embodiment of the woman who will change the world.

If not for us, then for our children.

And the time is now. Not tomorrow. Now.

Integration => Acceptance => Unity => Harmony

By integrating our feelings, we will remember what it's like to be a child and why we want to protect the children; we can perceive what is truth, love, and all that isn't truth, fear.

Once integrated, we begin to accept ourselves, accept each other and accept the world as it is. Only from this place can we make a difference. We can awaken from the dreamlike state of complacency, avoidance and numbness and see the reality of the situation.

We can see that our neighbor is not our enemy, but a mirror of us. To kill our neighbor is not the answer. To seek to understand the different lens that our neighbor sees the world through is the answer.

We can start to unite as one human family and live in peace. But it does not end there. If we are peaceful with one another yet not living in harmony with the earth, we will go extinct.

In embodying the mother, we must honor the sacred Mother. Our earth.

She told her story.

Out of place. An outcast in tenth grade at a charter school. Her girlfriend, also an outcast, attempted suicide.

"I admit I've cut myself. I blame myself for it. If I had only …"

I called her name, stopping her mid-sentence. "Do you still blame yourself?"

A look of pain crossed her face. She nodded. Yes.

"It's not your fault."

Her lip quivered. She looked away.

I called her name again. "It's not your fault. You did nothing wrong."

She squirmed, pulling back as if to avoid the words hurling toward her. Tears came to her eyes.

"Look at me. It's not your fault." My voice shook. My eyes filled with tears. I felt her pain. I felt her resistance. I felt her struggle to allow these words to penetrate her heart.

I'm volunteering at a high school for *Jeans 4 Justice*, an organization I previously mentioned whose mission is to end sexual violence in the world. I have a circle of a dozen tenth grade students and our topic is suicide.

Suicide. Hopelessness. Feeling like a failure. Feeling not good enough. Trapped. Seeing no way out.

I'd had a few friends attempt suicide. A few had asked me to help them get out of the hole they found themselves in. I was a rock for them, a safe space to talk about that deepest darkest shame that was swallowing them up. They felt my passion, my drive, my desire to live. I was their buoy, their raft, their life line.

The boy sitting next to me, her best friend, had tears in his eyes. I put my hand on his back. "These guys love you. You are amazing. Can you get this? You have done nothing wrong. You did the best you could. Tell her who she is for you."

With tears streaming down his face he looked at her. "I love you."

At this moment, I knew why I did what I did. I knew that everything in my life – all my training, all my events, all my work – had led to this point.

This was leadership.

Vulnerable.
Raw.
Painfully real.
Caring.
Compassionate.
Gentle.
Direct.
Heart ripped wide open.
Down to the core.
Connecting. Pulsing. Uncomfortable. Nauseous. Cathartic.
Life altering.
Freedom. Unity. Joy.

The shift.

It was all right there in that moment. Penetrating through the wall of the ego filled with fear, shame, guilt, blame and getting to the depth of the heart.

This is interconnectedness. This is how we build a new world through community.

These kids feel so alone. Helpless. Hopeless.

What the fuck can I do? A boy's words echoed through my head. *I beat the shit out of him for attempting suicide. I didn't know what else to do. It doesn't feel right, but I don't know what else to do.*

Our world is suffering. Humanity is in so much pain. I'm so clear that there is a way through this darkness to the light. Our children do not have to go through this. We can give them hope. We can give them vehicles to channel this energy they are feeling and do something positive with it.

It's Called Co-Creative Leadership.

When a spark lights a flame deep within our belly, that flicker of hope says, "I can make a difference. Maybe, just maybe, I can do something about this problem. Maybe, just maybe, I can be part of the solution. Maybe my experience was supposed to happen – I was supposed to go through this pain so that I can help others out from theirs. And through that process, I can know myself as a leader. And I don't have to do it alone. I am connected. I have community. I am supported. We can do this."

We were each given a life path with very specific lessons to learn along the way, to gain the tools necessary to live out our *dharma*. We were each born with unique gifts and unique circumstances. This is the diversity aspect. But we all have the same heart. We all experience the same emotions. We feel the same energy. It's what connects us. The life force. *Qi*. *Prana*. The breath. The heartbeat. The inexplicable synchronicities. The miracles that happen when we open our hearts and surrender. There is an essence of who we are as divine beings, souls in these human bodies, that knows that anything is possible. That has this power to co-create.

We resist the hell out of this power to co-create. We don't trust. We don't want to listen. It is so scary, so unknown, so inexplicable. And yet, this is the way through. To stop the pain and suffering, we must go through it, not around it. There is no avoiding it.

We are divine beings all having a human experience. The pain, no matter what the circumstance, is the same. The suffering, no matter why it is occurring, is the same. Our hearts yearn for connection. For peace. For love. For harmony.

And it's through Co-Creative Leadership that we can create our collective hearts' deepest desires.

The intention of this book is to awaken our souls to unite as one human family. To create community, one interconnected tribe, on the planet. Beautiful in its diversity. Magnificent in its capacity to overcome adversity. Powerful in its unlimited possibilities.

We can co-create an experience where people feel fulfilled with peace in their hearts, which gets reflected in the world around us.

The solution is simple. I'm not going to say it will be easy, but it boils down to one core belief that if we can embrace, will change the world.

It is:

I am enough. You are enough.
I am good enough exactly as I am. You are good enough exactly as you are.

There is nothing wrong with you. You have done nothing wrong. It's time to unlock your potential as a leader so that, together, we can *be* the change we wish to see in the world.

As the embodiment of the mother, life isn't about me anymore. I've always wanted to make a difference, serving from a place of "not good enough." I had to serve to feel like I mattered.

I'm no longer in that place. I get I am enough just as I am. And now I can truly serve other women, the children and the men of this planet from truth.

Sister Spotlight: Alison's Story

As a child, my biggest challenge was learning how to be in this world - not of it. And with a tender heart, this felt impossible. Even scary and frustrating. Because I didn't understand what I was actually feeling.

I was overwhelmed by one of my greatest gifts – my capacity to feel DEEPLY. And I didn't know what to do or who to be with such raw intensity and wild feelings.

I felt everyone, everything – the entire planet. All the time.

I was afraid of my humanity. Because I couldn't control it or change it. I felt helpless yet responsible for the world. And everyone in it.

I had so many questions...

"How was I supposed to help the world if I felt vulnerable and tender?"
"Wasn't I supposed to be strong and keep it together?"
"How could my tears contribute to the well-being of all?"
And most importantly, "How can I help here?"

I even remember bursting into tears telling my Mom "I think I came too early!" And my childhood companion, Mother Mary, would just smile at me. And say "All is well."

I can't even begin to tell you how many times I asked Mary for a book. A manual.

Something that told me how to be human! And she would say "Feel Alison. Feel."

So I would ask for more help. And more tears would flow. More feelings would arise. And I would say "Thank you."

My tenderness was often misunderstood. By myself and others. I was often thought of as "fragile," "too sensitive" or "too emotional." So I used to fight my tender heart, wishing I was tougher.

I even tried to hide her so I could fit in. But that didn't work because I couldn't keep Mary's love and beauty stuffed inside anymore.

It was exhausting. Confusing. Maddening. Incredibly sad. And it left me feeling disconnected from my greatest gifts and sense of personal power.

I felt obligated to protect and save my heart from hurt, pain or any part of life that seemed scary.

But here's what I quickly learned...

If my heart isn't able to freely express herself fully, that pain is often more intense and harmful than any other external or outside force.

Because the pain of holding back love and not receiving it or not tapping into its innate creative potential can be destructive and crippling to life. And not being free to feel without apology is suffocation for my Soul. So I decided I wouldn't allow shame to have a claim on my heart's most natural expression of Love any longer.

My heart is in touch with the Spirit of humanity. And always will be. She dives deep and feels even deeper. All emotions. The full spectrum.

My tender heart is a great spiritual gift. She knows how to feel and stays open to receive love. Which are essential elements to embracing my humanity.

When I joined in Sistership Circle, I was curious how my tenderness would be received. During our first circle, I expressed my intentions and desires. And bravely gave each woman permission to call me out if they saw me trying to hide any part of my Soul or spiritual gifts.

I also spoke up and said I needed our circle to be a safe place for my full multidimensional self to show up and be present. And with warm smiles and embracing hugs, each woman welcomed all of me.

With a few tears streaming down my cheeks, I knew my Spirit would receive and give nourishment in every form over the next 6 months and beyond.

I show up, fully present (tears and all) every circle. Ready to share from the heart. And receive support and encouragement for even fuller expression.

Being within a community where I receive abundant opportunities for sharing the depth of my heart is vital to my Soul's freedom of creative expression.

Knowing I have a sisterhood supporting my deepest desires helps me move forward in life with greater ease. It feeds my presence. And I have witnesses to hold me accountable to seeing it through.

All of me is welcome here. And I am grateful.

I live in tenderness. It's a brave place to live. One I dare to embrace each day.

My inner child's Spirit is already free. And liberated. Untamed and wild. On purpose. Alive with tenderness. Awake to her power as gentleness.

She doesn't need to be controlled, fixed or changed. Only accepted and nurtured. And raised into the fullness of her spiritual expression with compassion and unconditional love. It's the most important gift I can give myself and others.

I thrive in the kindness of allowing. It creates even more beauty and peace within my Soul.

I am grateful for my tender heart and the gifts she brings. I choose to celebrate her today. And *every* day.

I wasn't born to fit in, but to create a whole new world where my tenderness is leading the way home. I take a deep breath and trust. Melting into surrender, as I dwell in Peace.

Won't you come play?

Just follow your tenderness... it will lead the way.

I see and feel your heart and give thanks for the beauty you give into this world.

May you keep shining brightly and have the courage to feel. Our world needs more gentleness, kindness and compassion. And I thank you for yours.

~ Alison Elsberry

Inquiry Journaling/Affirming Rituals

1. What do you need to integrate within yourself to draw your line in the sand and create a new paradigm for the next generation?

2. Journal about unity and connection among the human family. Describe your *community* that supports your greatness.

Chapter 15: Like a Phoenix Out of the Ashes

"I am a new generation feminine leader."

Ever since this embodiment of the feminine, ripping open my heart, surrendering, softening, allowing, receiving, I've been asking myself what I'm supposed to do with my fire.

I was so driven before to take action. I wanted to save and change the world. I wanted to make massive impact. I recognize now that it was coming from a wounded place of proving to myself and others that I matter and my life is worth living.

I believed that the measure of my worthiness was based on what I was doing in the world and the amount of success I had in achieving my dreams.

So no matter what goal I reached, it felt unfulfilling. Unsatisfying. An unquenchable thirst. My mouth dry, my stomach hungry. More. More. More.

I remember the day one of my tribe leaders asked me what success looked like to me with Tribal Truth. I responded: a global network of tribes, all working in connection and collaboration with one another. She responded: you realize you are already doing that? I made excuses that we were "global" only in the sense that there was one international city – London – in the network. Vancouver had folded. We didn't even have ten tribes at that point. So it felt too small. Technically, I had reached my goal, but it didn't feel like it was enough. I realized that it would never be enough. And in this masculine model of conquering the world, I would never be enough.

So I descended into the feminine. Falling. Arms flailing. Anxious, fearful, panic stricken. It was a scary point in my life and I fought against surrendering, holding tightly onto whatever I thought I knew about myself and the world.

I didn't understand or see what was going on because I felt like I was in a dark tunnel with no view of the other side. No light. Complete darkness. I felt my way through, hoping, praying for the other side that I would come out of.

In the darkest part of the tunnel, I could barely get out of bed. I would go completely unconscious, passing out in my clothes and waking up confused of what happened or when I fell asleep. All I wanted to do was sleep. I was just so tired. All I cared about was laying down in my bed in the comfort of being swaddled in blankets like a baby. Cocooned. Safe. Nurtured.

"Working" as I knew it before was not an option. I needed to do as little as possible. Luckily, I had one group of women who I "led" in a mastermind at this time, my financial support so that I could be in this dark place.

And as I "survived" with more than enough money to live, I came to see that I really didn't need to do anything. I came to see the truth that I mattered, I was enough, doing the bare minimum. I stopped judging myself. I stopped chasing the money. I stopped being busy. I simply stopped.

Oh space. Spacious time. Spacious afternoons to lie in bed from 1-5 pm. Permission to sleep. Permission to do absolutely nothing. Permission to be.

I am choked up thinking about this … how much we are chasing the dream … but whose dream? And when are we going to wake up and see that it is all an illusion?

- The illusion that we have to do everything and be super woman to matter.
- The illusion that we have to get a job and be successful and our worth is based on how much money we make.
- The illusion that the material world is all there is and so we must collect and accumulate as much stuff as possible.
- The illusion that we have to save the world.
- The illusion that there is something to fix and change.
- The illusion that there is something wrong with us.

As I gave myself space, I noticed there was this trail of incompletions behind me. It was like a trail of breadcrumbs leading back to my childhood. My job was to go back and pick up those pieces that I had left behind. To integrate all these parts of myself that I judged and discarded. So I did. The past just kept showing up in my present moment life and I couldn't look away. I had to face all the "demons" that I had shut away in the closet. And as I shed light on each demon, I became stronger in my core. I felt myself regaining strength. I felt myself recollected, whole, complete.

People from my past showed up in droves. Memories resurfaced. I cried and cried, feeling the grief that I stuffed down all these years. I had been running all over the world, trying to find myself, building community to feel worthy and important, and the truth was, I didn't need to run anymore. *I had finally come home to myself.*

This was the path of self-acceptance. I suddenly found myself in the shoes of the people I had judged over the years and I had a new sense of acceptance and compassion for others.

The more I accepted, the more I loved. My heart continued to open more and more, increasing my capacity for love. Love for myself. Love for others.

With this new knowing inside of me, I felt my fire. I felt Kali arising in me.

Kali has been my goddess archetype since 2007 and she's shown up in many forms in my life.

If you haven't heard of this Hindu goddess, she is usually depicted with multiple limbs holding weapons, a necklace of heads around her neck, her bloody tongue hanging out of her mouth, and her foot standing on the chest of a dead man beneath her.

That dead man was the God Shiva, who she accidentally killed when he came to stop her rampage and she couldn't identify him in her rage.

This rage at the world is not the way we will save or change the world.

This eye for an eye, get revenge attitude is just perpetuating the problem.

This is not the new Co-Creative Leadership model.

It is okay to be angry and it is okay to be fiercely bitchy when attacked. But it is not okay to rage and project that anger onto someone else and hurt (or even kill) him in the process.

We have so much to be angry about. We should feel that rage. The years of being shut down and shut up. The years of suppression and violence against women. Most of us were oppressed at some point in history. Not only that, but millions of people are suffering in the world today with malnutrition and unsanitary living conditions. Corporations continue to wreak havoc on communities and get away with it.

Enough. No more. We will not tolerate this behavior. We will not enable it.

In *Mighty Be Our Powers*, Leymah Gbowee demonstrates what Kali looks like embodied in new feminine leadership. She rallied 200 women outside the Liberia negotiation hall in 2003 and refused to let any of the men leaders out until they signed a peace treaty. She was enraged.

Furious. She was not taking no for an answer. She threatened to strip down and bare her breast, the ultimate insult to a man in that culture.

But in threatening to strip, I had summoned up a traditional power. In Africa, it's a terrible curse to see a married or elderly woman deliberately bare herself. If a mother is really, really upset with a child, she might take out her breast and slap it, and he's cursed. For this group of men to see a woman naked would be almost like a death sentence. Men are born through women's vaginas, and it's as if by exposing ourselves, we say, "We now take back the life we gave you." Fear passed through the hall. [22]

She didn't use force. She didn't use violence. She channeled that anger and rage into a stand so great that the power of the feminine was felt by the men and they surrendered.

She literally just stood there and opened her flower petals.

The world right now is governed in a way that is out of harmony with the earth. The system built by man is on the brink of collapse. Trillions of dollars are pumped into the war machine. At the press of a button, we can all be POOF gone. The nuclear war threat is imminent. We know there is a "problem" and the big question is "what are we going to do about it?"

We're not going to fight against it.
We're not going to judge anyone as bad or wrong.
We're not going to go to war.

That's all the same conversation. The same outcome. More of the same thing. It is in resistance with the flow. It is going to perpetuate the problem.

We, as women, are being called to embody a new way of being, the feminine. And that means that we are all being called to stop the madness of running around in circles trying to prove that we can fit in with a model that is out of alignment and out of harmony with the natural flow of life.

We are being called to strip down, let go, surrender. We are being called to simply BE the feminine. To inspire simply by who we are being. And then stand together, as Leymah did, in sisterhood with one another, in Co-Creative Leadership, and to have that stand be so inspirational that the war stops.

To take a stand.

To take a stand for our children to live in a world that nurtures them, that is safe to play in.

To take a stand for us to unite as one human family.

To take a stand for us to live in harmony with the earth.

Leymah didn't necessarily DO anything. She channeled that Kali energy and stood in her conviction. She inspired through her strength. She was a beacon of light. She stripped down to her essence and activated the truth.

I have swung from one side of the spectrum to the other. I've gone from the extreme masculine get-it-done mentality to the extreme feminine and found myself resting in the middle.

Integrated.

Balanced.

Using the energy and fire of Kali to burn through my own ignorance, awaken to my own truth, and come to a realization that I don't have to do anything except be unconditional love.

Choosing love above all else.

To choose is an action. To be love is an action. It is not passive. It requires *attention* and *intention*. *Attention* on the emotions arising in my body, the active choice to observe them, feel them fully, and allow them to pass through. *Intention* to not react in fear or anger. *Intention* to be centered, grounded, and calm in the midst of the storm.

When we choose love, we say no to fear.

When we choose love, we take a stand.

Choosing love starts within. Self-love.

All of us want to be loved. We all want to feel like we are enough, just as we are. If we can see that we are all acting like little children trying to get that love and attention from one another, we can start to develop the compassion and acceptance so desperately needed on our planet.

The wars today are like the fights on the playground. Grown men acting out the suppressed feelings that they felt as five-year-olds. Grown men unable to effectively communicate the lack of safety they feel because they don't feel loved. Dominate, control, and manipulate to get what they want. The desire for power is an acting out to feel worthy. It comes from fear and scarcity. The power struggle comes from the illusion of separation and the fear of getting hurt. I'll hurt you before you hurt me. It's all coming from insecurity as a five-year-old. Angry, afraid and hurt little boys pretending to be men.

The thing that stops us in our tracks and actually makes us think about our actions is when we think about our children. We see the innocence, the play, the joy, the love. The truth is, there is no separation between us and our children. We are them. We have simply forgotten our own innocence. We have suppressed and shut down our own inner child, the little girl inside of us who feels so deeply.

To make a difference, to change the world, we, as women, must allow ourselves to feel our little girls crying out. We must listen to them. We must love them. We must protect them. We must embody the divine mother for ourselves first and then embody the divine mother for our children and the earth.

There is a process at work here to embody the mother.

Death.
Crossing the threshold.
Stepping into Spiritual Adulthood.

As I integrated my childhood emotions, I had to let go of those admonitions. I had to purify myself. I had to kill them, burn them, destroy them. I had to go to war internally.

Those beliefs are not mine. They never were.

That fire burning inside of me became a raging flame, stoked by my anger at these things that suppressed me. These things that were not mine.

The illusions held onto so tightly by the ego must die.

The old must die for the new to be born.

Death is not a bad thing. It is not evil. It is not something to fear. It is inevitable. It is part of the cycle of life. It is a necessary part of the process to transition from the old to the new paradigm.

Like a phoenix out of the ashes, you cross the threshold into being a Spiritual Adult. One who can unconditionally love herself, and spread that love to everyone else.

There is nothing to fear. You have nothing to lose. It starts with you. It starts from within. Celebrate this moment without thinking about making the next grandiose plan for the future. Celebrate who you are, what you've done, where you are today.

If we don't revel in this moment, drink it in, sit in it, celebrate it, we miss the entire point.

Let go of the past and future and breathe in the moment.

Just breathe.

This is the person who you have always wanted to be. This is the self-reliant, self-responsible, self-reflective and self-respecting adult who leads in truth and love.

Leading your life in flow with least effort.

This is who embodies Co-Creative Leadership.

History will repeat itself over and over again until we get the message. The message is through integration. The message is to let go of the illusion. The message is to literally kill this old identity that we, as humans, continue to play over and over again.

Over and over again.

This is not about fixing, changing or converting. This is about getting real about what's really going on. To face ourselves once and for all and take a look at the shadow and cast a light on it.

To end the internal battle that wages on. To step into Embodiment. Knowing. Truth.

Be the light worker.
Be the change.

It comes back to you loving yourself, accepting yourself, being yourself. This model is what we pass down to the next generation, our children, who need a new model of leadership.

I am ...

Bold enough to use my **voice** for good.
Courageous enough to **admit** when I'm wrong.
Strong enough to be **vulnerable**.
Audacious enough to **love** someone who hates.
Daring enough to **accept** someone who's done me wrong.
Tough enough to wear my **heart** on my sleeve.
Resolute enough to **take care** of my body.
Risky enough to **forgive**.
Undaunted enough to take a **stand**.

And I am taking a stand that we join together as one tribe on the planet right now so that future generations can look back and thank us for the work we've done in collaboration.

Sister Spotlight: Sage's Story

I am an enigma. I have spent my life making it look good on the outside, appearing as if I have it all together, succeeding in the eyes of the world, embodying my masculine. People who don't know me don't ask why I live this way. There are very few who do know me really, and they don't ask why I've lived that way- they know why.

Since I came into this world, I was different. Other kids were curious, adults sometimes looked at me askance; my own parents didn't know quite what to do with me. I was wired differently. I was born clairvoyant to parents who couldn't conceptualize that there was a world beyond the one they could touch and feel. I learned slowly but surely to hide my gifts as others didn't respond well to their inclusion. The secret burned inside me, desperately desiring to be shared with others, isolating me, leaving me without a natural tribe.

While my singularity wasn't hard initially, eventually it made me a target. Just as predators learn to separate an animal from the herd in order to hunt it, my isolation made me visible to predators in my community. By the time I was seven, I had been brutally raped by an older sibling of one of my few friends, and assaulted by a baby sitter. I recoiled inside myself. I didn't know who to tell. I didn't know what to say. Everything and everyone seemed dangerous to the little girl that I was, so in the silence, I left that little girl behind on a beach and told her I'd be back when it was safe.

By the time I was fifteen, I was targeted by a local cartel. Groomed by one of the drug dealers and completely oblivious to what was happening, I thought the dashing young man liked me. I thought I was his girlfriend. Turns out I had value, but not the kind that you'd ever want to have. I became a party favor for his clients, without the power to make my own choices, or even to maintain boundaries for my body. He forced me to use cocaine, muddying my already dulled senses, making me an unwitting accomplice to their activities.

At seventeen, I became pregnant. While frightened and unsure how I would be able to manage, I envisioned a life with Emily. I saw her as the one good thing that would come from this shadow world of which I'd become a part. But, only a few months into the pregnancy, my handler became enraged with me. I was beside myself and swallowed a bottle of pills. In less than twenty minutes, my heart stopped and I crossed over. After a complex Out of Body Experience (OBE), I was yanked by the Silver Cord and pulled back into my body, gasping for air. Confused and scared, I was propelled into the bathroom and emptied the contents of my stomach. I survived but Emily did not. Just days later, I miscarried, and it felt as if there was nothing left to live for.

I don't know how I survived that life but I always knew that I had angels surrounding me. I may not have had a human tribe, but I had a Divine one.

During the course of the next thirty years, I performed miracles repeatedly as life dealt me one blow after another. Time after time, I endured horrific circumstances, illnesses and injuries. Eight times, my heart stopped and somehow I returned to the land of the living. I became a force to be reckoned with in my Divine Masculine, but with every new painful experience, my Divine Feminine was safeguarded deeper and deeper inside me … until I found my tribe.

I had heard about a woman who was bringing women together—creating tribes for those who had become disconnected, disenfranchised and separate from their friends and family. After a year, on New Year's Eve, I finally met Tanya in the parking lot of a local store. Less than a week later, she'd sent me an invitation to a Sistership Circle that she was facilitating. I didn't know what I was saying yes to, but I graciously accepted her offer.

Nearly a year and three circles later, I have found my tribe -- not just external, but internal as well.

After a lifetime of running, superficial connection, and safeguarding my Divine Feminine, I have found a group of women with whom the connection is so deep that I have finally been able to battle my demons, embrace my shadows and my Light, and embody *all* that I am. I have journeyed to the beach and held that little girl perched at shore's edge, and have integrated her into the woman that I have become. I have shared my darkest secrets, my most painful truths and have stripped away all that keeps me from myself and from them.

Like a phoenix, I have risen from the ashes of that life, and now stride into all that awaits me in this incarnation, my tribe at my side.

~ Sage Breslin

Inquiry Journaling/Affirming Rituals

1. Journal about where in your life you will take a stand. How *brilliantly audacious* will you be?

Closing Ritual

Close your eyes and take a deep breath in. Fill up your lungs with air and then let it go, allowing all of your worries, doubts and fears to disappear.

Breathe in again and, this time, feel the love from your sisters all around you. When you release the breath, surrender into the arms of your sisters. Allow them to hold you. Imagine their hands on your back. Press into it. Feel the support.

On the third and final breath in, feel the joy rising in your belly. When you exhale, let out a sigh of relief that you are on this planet right here right now. Thank God you are alive.

Three breaths. The holy trinity.

Earth, sun and moon.
Body, mind and spirit.
Mother, Daughter and Sister.

You, me, and the world.

We are in this journey together and it is just the beginning.

The moment you get overwhelmed, remember to breathe. Just be. YOU.

*Creating a feminine container to hold the world
to inspire and empower the masculine.*

About the Author

Tanya Lynn is a "strategic activator" — gifted at coaching women to soar to new heights by putting together a plan that maximizes their talents and strengths and taking bold, courageous actions to fulfill on their intentions.

Tanya is the visionary CEO behind the international organization, Sistership Circle, a worldwide sisterhood movement empowering women to step into their true beauty, brilliance and boldness as feminine leaders. She started training facilitators to use her proven 12-week Circle Program based on her bestselling book "Open Your Heart: How to be a New Generation Feminine Leader. She is also the author of "How to Lead Circle."

She is a respected leader in the industry from clients and colleagues alike because she's the real deal, living and breathing her work.

She believes that the new model of feminine leadership is not about hierarchies of power but about circles of collaboration. For us to become true leaders, we must embrace our sisters as our allies and give one another permission to shine. Learn more at sistershipcircle.com.

Acknowledgments

I almost threw out this book halfway through the editing process. I knew birthing a book was difficult, but I didn't think I would be so resistant when it was in the birth canal!

My first acknowledgement is for the three women in my mastermind who turned everything around for me on one of our calls. Thank you Brenda Chapman, Jordanna Eyre and especially Jennifer Horton for giving me the inspirational reflections that helped me find the courage to fully surrender and allow the book to just simply be.

This book would also not have been possible without the hundreds of Tribal Truth members who I have learned so much from. I have a deep appreciation for these women's courage to lean into their vulnerability and be in partnership with one another. Everything in this book comes from my interactions with these women. Big acknowledgement to Novalena for being my greatest teacher and mirror.

Thank you Lori Sortino for introducing me to Long Dance, which was a catalyst for the Honoring The Masculine events. I am so grateful for the men who later showed up at those events and especially to John and Mike for diving headfirst with me into the masculine-feminine dance. You have altered my relationship with the masculine forever.

One man in particular, Barry Green, was an instrumental part of my journey in 2013. His guidance empowered me to heal the mother wound and surrender into the feminine. Because of him, I trust like I've never trusted before. He helped me fall in love with myself and embody the divine feminine.

To my Women's Mastermind of Carlsbad: thank you Jenn, Wendy, Priscilla, Beth, Suki, Susan, Talyn, Dale and Christina for your constant love and support. You allowed me to fall apart, get messy and just be. You held me as I built my foundation in the feminine.

To my women's circles: thank you Isabella, Corinne, Rivka, Sophia, Leora, Maire Claire, Maggie, Ilana, Candice, Frieda, Chrissy, Becca, Andrea, Kelsey, Sarah, Paula, Diane, and Kelly for your partnership and believing in me.

One woman in particular, Deborah Brown, was an absolute rockstar in editing, structuring and managing the publishing of this book. You gave me the strength to keep going when I wanted to quit. You blew me away with your generosity of time and effort. Thank you for your enthusiasm, support and stand for this book to be published.

Thank you to my sisters who partnered with me to make my vision to bring men and women together a reality: Laura Swan, Jess Johnson, Michele Rooney, Lucia Nicola Evans, Christina Dunbar, Galit Szolomowicz, Sabrina Chaw, Jan Robinson, and Marta Maria Marraccini.

Jodi Komitor, Anat Peri, Christina Dunbar and Sammy Caplan: you have unconditionally loved me through this process and I appreciate your sisterhood. When I didn't believe in myself, you reflected my greatness so I could believe in myself.

And last but not least, my tribe leaders who stuck with me through thick and thin, teaching me that co-creative leadership really works: Johanna Lyman, Jessica Tomlinson, Jessica Libbey, Claire Brummell, Brenda Chapman and Maria Merloni. These ladies showed me what the three C's of Tribe look like in action. I love you so much.

ACKNOWLEDGMENTS

Of course, this acknowledgment section would not be complete without thanking my mom for always being so open. You are a rock and the embodiment of the Queen. I'm so lucky to be your daughter.

Resources and Citations

1. Seven Generation Sustainability
2. Four Years Go - Overview
3. Worst Natural Disasters - Outdoor Life
4. Non GMO Project - Learn More
5. Tarot Card Meanings - Biddy Tarot
6. Sustainability - Wikipedia
7. Four Years Go - Solutions
8. Millenium Development Article - Marianne Williamson in Huff Post
9. About Hypothyroidism
10. Julia Cameron, The Artist's Way (2002-03-04)
11. Surprising Facts about Orgasm - Woman's Day
12. Side Effects of Depoprovera - Livestrong
13. Body Wisdom Healing
14. Poverty Income - CNN
15. Credit Card Debt - Money
16. Global Rise of Female Entrepreneurs
17. M. Scott Peck (2010-05-11). *The Different Drum: Community Making and Peace* (Kindle Locations 1501-1503). Touchstone. Kindle Edition.
18. Strengths Finder
19. Enneagram Institute
20. Connecting with Colors
21. Long Dance
22. Leymah Gbowee (2011-09-13), *Mighty Be Our Powers: How Sisterhood, Prayer, and Sex Changed a Nation at War* (p. 162). Beast Books. Kindle Edition.